ISBN 0-8373-6901-0
129D ADMISSION TEST SERIES

New **RUDMAN'S QUESTIONS AND ANSWERS ON THE...**

AASSWB/IV

American Association of State Social Work Boards

Examination in Social Work/ Clinical

Intensive preparation for the examination including...

- Human Development & Behavior
- Issues of Diversity
- Diagnosis & Assessment
- Psychotherapy & Clinical Practice
- Communication
- The Therapeutic Relationship
- Professional Values & Ethics
- Clinical Supervision, Consultation & Staff Development
- Practice Evaluation & Utilization of Research
- Service Delivery
- Clinical Practice & Management in the Organizational Setting

NATIONAL LEARNING CORPORATION

Copyright © 2007 by

National Learning Corporation

212 Michael Drive, Syosset, New York 11791

(516) 921-8888
(800) 645-6337
FAX: (516) 921-8743
www.passbooks.com
sales @ passbooks.com
info @ passbooks.com

PRINTED IN THE UNITED STATES OF AMERICA

PASSBOOK®
NOTICE

PASSBOOK SERIES®

THE *PASSBOOK SERIES®* has been created to prepare applicants and candidates for the ultimate academic battlefield – the examination room.

At some time in our lives, each and every one of us may be required to take an examination – for validation, matriculation, admission, qualification, registration, certification, or licensure.

Based on the assumption that every applicant or candidate has met the basic formal educational standards, has taken the required number of courses, and read the necessary texts, the *PASSBOOK SERIES®* furnishes the one special preparation which may assure passing with confidence, instead of failing with insecurity. Examination questions – together with answers – are furnished as the basic vehicle for study so that the mysteries of the examination and its compounding difficulties may be eliminated or diminished by a sure method.

This book is meant to help you pass your examination provided that you qualify and are serious in your objective.

The entire field is reviewed through the huge store of content information which is succinctly presented through a provocative and challenging approach – the question-and-answer method.

A climate of success is established by furnishing the correct answers at the end of each test.

You soon learn to recognize types of questions, forms of questions, and patterns of questioning. You may even begin to anticipate expected outcomes.

You perceive that many questions are repeated or adapted so that you can gain acute insights, which may enable you to score many sure points.

You learn how to confront new questions, or types of questions, and to attack them confidently and work out the correct answers.

You note objectives and emphases, and recognize pitfalls and dangers, so that you may make positive educational adjustments.

Moreover, you are kept fully informed in relation to new concepts, methods, practices, and directions in the field.

You discover that you are actually taking the examination all the time: you are preparing for the examination by "taking" an examination, not by reading extraneous and/or supererogatory textbooks.

In short, this PASSBOOK®, used directedly, should be an important factor in helping you to pass your test.

AASSWB EXAMINATIONS IN SOCIAL WORK

The examination

90 - 107
Correct
Needed.

How many questions are on the examination?

There are 170 questions on the AASSWB examination, but only 150 count toward your score. The remaining 20 are pretest items, questions which are being evaluated for possible inclusion in the examination item pool.

How much time will I have to take it?

You will have four hours to complete the examination. If you have special needs which fall under the Americans with Disabilities Act (ADA), you may be allotted extra time. Check your candidate handbook for details on how to arrange for special accommodations.

What is the passing score?

The raw passing score—that is, how many questions you need to have answered correctly in order to pass the examination—varies from administration to administration. Your jurisdiction's scaled score, however, will remain constant. Individual administrations are equated to account for slight variations in the difficulty of individual items.

Is the same test administered all year?

No. There are multiple versions, or forms, of each level of the AASSWB examination, and within those forms, the order of items is changed frequently. Some items will be the same from one administration to the next, but all items are reordered as part of the new examination.

Are the examinations at some administrations easier than at others?

No. Strictly speaking, the difficulty of the individual questions in a particular administration may vary, since the actual questions vary. But this variation is taken into account in the passing score required in any particular administration. If an administration shows a lower initial difficulty level, for example, the number of correct responses required to pass will be raised. In that sense, overall difficulty remains constant.

What are the examination versions?

Currently, there are four versions of examination offered by AASSWB. The Basic examination was designed to test the social work knowledge necessary at entry for social workers with the BSW degree. The Intermediate examination has been targeted for social workers with the MSW degree who have les than two years of practice experience. The Advanced and Clinical examinations test entry-level knowledge for social workers holding the MSW degree with at least two years of post-degree practice experience.

Are the tests the same from state to state?

Yes. Keep in mind, however, that every jurisdiction chooses the examination levels to be administered, so not every jurisdiction offers every level. The examination levels themselves are the same—the Clinical level AASSWB examination in Illinois, for example, is the same as the Clinical level AASSWB examination administered in California. That is where the similarities end--test: are not equivalent between levels (for example, the Intermediate level examina tion is not equivalent to the Basic, Clinical or Advanced level examinations).

Is this examination really a valid test of my social work knowledge?

Yes. The AASSWB examinations meet the testing standards established by tl American Psychological Association. AASSWB and its testing vendor monitc the validity and reliability of each test administered.

Who writes the questions?

Social work practitioners across the country submit potential items for the AASSWB item pool. Some of these practitioners are item writers specially contracted by the association to write and edit test questions. Other items are developed through item-writing workshops attended by volunteers. All exami nation items must meet with the approval of the AASSWB Examination Committee before being pretested. All examination items are pretested before they are included as official scored items.

Besides this guide, what courses or preparatory materials does AASSWB endorse?

The American Association of State Social Work Boards does not endorse any study course or materials designed to prepare you for the social work examination. There is no guarantee that the content of these study courses is related to the content of the AASSWB examinations.

Test administration

Do I have to know how to use a computer to take this examination?

No. Although the AASSWB examination is administered through a computer, it requires no previous computer experience. The equipment will allow you to skip questions and return to them, change your answers, and flag questions for later review. You will be given a brief tutorial on the operation of the computer.

I have a disability. Can I receive special accommodations?

Yes. By filling out an ADA form (available from your jurisdiction's board) you can qualify for accommodations under the Americans with Disabilities Act (ADA).

How do I register to take the examination?

Always begin by checking with your jurisdiction's social work board, and then check your candidate handbook. If you have difficulties finding out who to call, phone AASSWB at (800) 225-6880 for contact listings in your jurisdiction.

Is the examination offered in languages other than English?

No. But many states do allow special accommodations for candidates whose primary language is something other than English. Contact your board for information.

Scores and score reporting

If I pass the test in one jurisdiction, have I passed it in all jurisdictions?

Yes, providing the other jurisdictions accept the examination level you've taken. The passing score for the AASSWB examination is a national passing score. That does not mean you are automatically licensed across the country—every jurisdiction has its own licensing processes, and there are additional steps that must be taken in order to gain licensure. Always check with the social work boards for details.

If I fail the test in one jurisdiction, have I failed it in all jurisdictions?

Yes. For the same reason that passing scores are national scores, scores lower than passing remain so across all jurisdictions that use the AASSWB examinations.

Will I get to know how many items I answered correctly?

No. Your score reports will show your performance as a scaled score, which does not reflect the number of items you answered correctly. Similarly, the diagnostic reports supplied to failed candidates only provide a general evaluation of performance, and do not supply specific performance statistics.

Can I get my score over the phone?

No. In order to protect the confidentiality of all licensure candidates, score reports are never given out over the telephone.

If I fail the examination, how long before I can take it again?

The waiting period between retakes can vary, but the minimum wait is 90 days. Check with your jurisdiction to verify the retake schedule.

How many times can I retake the examination?

That depends on your jurisdiction. Many have limits on how many times candidates can retake the test.

AASSWB CLINICAL LEVEL EXAMINATION

As mentioned earlier, the AASSWB examinations are based on specific content outlines. The content outline for the AASSWB examination is provided here as a tool for your review. Remember, to figure out just how many questions will make up the various content areas, simply multiply the percentages by 150.

Outline for the Clinical examination

These content areas were developed through the task analysis conducted among licensed social workers in many practice settings. The outline reflects groupings of the knowledge areas that are linked directly to the test items.

% of Test		
17%	I.	**Human Development and Behavior**
		A. Theories of human development and behavior
		B. Normal development in the life cycle of individuals, families, and groups
		C. Human behavior
		D. Impact of crises and changes
		E. Family functioning
		F. Addictions
		G. Abuse and neglect
5%	II.	**Issues of Diversity**
		A. Effects of culture, race, and/or ethnicity
		B. Effects of sexual orientation and/or gender
		C. Effects of age and/or disability
12%	III.	**Diagnosis and Assessment**
		A. Assessment
		B. Information gathering
		C. Diagnostic classifications
		D. Indicators of abuse and neglect
		E. Indicators of danger to self and others
19%	IV.	**Psychotherapy and Clinical Practice**
		A. Intervention theories and models
		B. The intervention process
		C. Treatment planning

		D. Intervention techniques
		E. Intervention with couples and families
		F. Intervention with groups

9%   **V.   Communication**
- A. Concepts and theories of communication
- B. Communication techniques

8%   **VI. The Therapeutic Relationship**
- A. Relationship theories
- B. Relationship practice

11%   **VII. Professional Values and Ethics**
- A. Value issues
- B. Legal and ethical issues
- C. Confidentiality

3%   **VIII.Clinical Supervision, Consultation, and Staff Development**
- A. Social work supervision
- B. Consultation and interdisciplinary collaboration
- C. Staff development

3%   **IX. Practice Evaluation and Utilization of Research**
- A. Evaluation techniques
- B. Utilization of research

9%   **X.   Service Delivery**
- A. Policies and procedures of service delivery
- B. Processes of service delivery

5%   **XI. Clinical Practice and Management in the Organizational Setting**
- A. Advocacy
- B. Finance
- C. Management and human resource issues

HOW TO TAKE A TEST

You have studied long, hard and conscientiously.

With your official admission card in hand, and your heart pounding, you have been admitted to the examination room.

You note that there are several hundred other applicants in the examination room waiting to take the same test.

They all appear to be equally well prepared.

You know that nothing but your best effort will suffice. The "moment of truth" is at hand: you now have to demonstrate objectively, in writing, your knowledge of content and your understanding of subject matter.

You are fighting the most important battle of your life—to pass and/or score high on an examination which will determine your career and provide the economic basis for your livelihood.

What extra, special things should you know and should you do in taking the examination?

BEFORE THE TEST

YOUR PHYSICAL CONDITION IS IMPORTANT

    If you are not well, you can't do your best work on tests. If you are half asleep, you can't do your best either. Here are some tips:

1) Get about the same amount of sleep you usually get. Don't stay up all night before the test, either partying or worrying—DON'T DO IT!
2) If you wear glasses, be sure to wear them when you go to take the test. This goes for hearing aids, too.
3) If you have any physical problems that may keep you from doing your best, be sure to tell the person giving the test. If you are sick or in poor health, you really cannot do your best on any test. You can always come back and take the test some other time.

AT THE TEST

EXAMINATION TECHNIQUES

1) Read the general instructions carefully. These are usually printed on the first page of the exam booklet. As a rule, these instructions refer to the timing of the examination; the fact that you should not start work until the signal and must stop work at a signal, etc. If there are any *special* instructions, such as a choice of questions to be answered, make sure that you note this instruction carefully.

2) When you are ready to start work on the examination, that is as soon as the signal has been given, read the instructions to each question booklet, underline any key words or phrases, such as *least, best, outline, describe* and the like. In this way you will tend to answer as requested rather than discover on reviewing your paper that you *listed without describing*, that you selected the *worst* choice rather than the *best* choice, etc.

3) If the examination is of the objective or multiple-choice type – that is, each question will also give a series of possible answers: A, B, C or D, and you are called upon to select the best answer and write the letter next to that answer on your answer paper – it is advisable to start answering each question in turn. There may be anywhere from 50 to 100 such questions in the three or four hours allotted and you can see how much time would be taken if you read through all the questions before beginning to answer any. Furthermore, if you come across a question or group of questions which you know would be difficult to answer, it would undoubtedly affect your handling of all the other questions.

4) If the examination is of the essay type and contains but a few questions, it is a moot point as to whether you should read all the questions before starting to answer any one. Of course, if you are given a choice – say five out of seven and the like – then it is essential to read all the questions so you can eliminate the two which are most difficult. If, however, you are asked to answer all the questions, there may be danger in trying to answer the easiest one first because you may find that you will spend too much time on it. The best technique is to answer the first question, then proceed to the second, etc.

5) Time your answers. Before the exam begins, write down the time it started, then add the time allowed for the examination and write down the time it must be completed, then divide the time available somewhat as follows:
   - If 3-1/2 hours are allowed, that would be 210 minutes. If you have 80 objective-type questions, that would be an average of 2-1/2 minutes per question. Allow yourself no more than 2 minutes per question, or a total of 160 minutes, which will permit about 50 minutes to review.
   - If for the time allotment of 210 minutes there are 7 essay questions to answer, that would average about 30 minutes a question. Give yourself only 25 minutes per question so that you have about 35 minutes to review.

6) The most important instruction is to *read each question* and make sure you know what is wanted. The second most important instruction is to *time yourself properly* so that you answer every question. The third most important instruction is to *answer every question*. Guess if you have to but include something for each question. Remember that you will receive no credit for a blank and will probably receive some credit if you write something in answer to an essay question. If you guess a letter – say "B" for a multiple-choice question – you may have guessed right. If you leave a blank as an answer to a multiple-choice question, the examiners may respect your

feelings but it will not add a point to your score. Some exams may penalize you for wrong answers, so in such cases *only*, you may not want to guess unless you have some basis for your answer.

7) Suggestions
   a. Objective-type questions
      1. Examine the question booklet for proper sequence of pages and questions
      2. Read all instructions carefully
      3. Skip any question which seems too difficult; return to it after all other questions have been answered
      4. Apportion your time properly; do not spend too much time on any single question or group of questions
      5. Note and underline key words – *all, most, fewest, least, best, worst, same, opposite,* etc.
      6. Pay particular attention to negatives
      7. Note unusual option, e.g., unduly long, short, complex, different or similar in content to the body of the question
      8. Observe the use of "hedging" words – *probably, may, most likely,* etc.
      9. Make sure that your answer is put next to the same number as the question
      10. Do not second-guess unless you have good reason to believe the second answer is definitely more correct
      11. Cross out original answer if you decide another answer is more accurate; do not erase until you are ready to hand your paper in
      12. Answer all questions; guess unless instructed otherwise
      13. Leave time for review

   b. Essay questions
      1. Read each question carefully
      2. Determine exactly what is wanted. Underline key words or phrases.
      3. Decide on outline or paragraph answer
      4. Include many different points and elements unless asked to develop any one or two points or elements
      5. Show impartiality by giving pros and cons unless directed to select one side only
      6. Make and write down any assumptions you find necessary to answer the questions
      7. Watch your English, grammar, punctuation and choice of words
      8. Time your answers; don't crowd material

8) Answering the essay question

Most essay questions can be answered by framing the specific response around several key words or ideas. Here are a few such key words or ideas:

M's: manpower, materials, methods, money, management
P's: purpose, program, policy, plan, procedure, practice, problems, pitfalls, personnel, public relations

a. Six basic steps in handling problems:
   1. Preliminary plan and background development
   2. Collect information, data and facts
   3. Analyze and interpret information, data and facts
   4. Analyze and develop solutions as well as make recommendations
   5. Prepare report and sell recommendations
   6. Install recommendations and follow up effectiveness

b. Pitfalls to avoid
   1. *Taking things for granted* – A statement of the situation does not necessarily imply that each of the elements is necessarily true; for example, a complaint may be invalid and biased so that all that can be taken for granted is that a complaint has been registered
   2. *Considering only one side of a situation* – Wherever possible, indicate several alternatives and then point out the reasons you selected the best one
   3. *Failing to indicate follow up* – Whenever your answer indicates action on your part, make certain that you will take proper follow-up action to see how successful your recommendations, procedures or actions turn out to be
   4. *Taking too long in answering any single question* – Remember to time your answers properly

EXAMINATION SECTION

EXAMINATION SECTION
TEST 1

Directions: Each question or incomplete statement is followed by several suggested answers or completions. Select the one the BEST answers the question or completes the statement. *PRINT THE LETTER OF THE CORRECT ANSWER IN THE SPACE AT THE RIGHT.*

1) Which of the following statements about working with elderly clients in therapy is TRUE?

1.

A. Cognitive approaches are usually contraindicated because of the cognitive demands placed on the client.
B. Elderly clients often become over-dependent on the therapist due to their relative isolation and loneliness.
C. The therapeutic relationship may be more difficult to form than it would with younger clients
D. Insight-oriented therapies are usually contraindicated because of the cognitive impairments that typically accompany aging.

2) A 45-year-old client reports to a clinician for an initial consultation upon the advice of her physician. The client complains of headaches, neck pain, stomach and lower back pain, and dizziness. After an initial examination, the client's physician has failed to find any physiological cause for his problems. Which of the following conditions would justify a diagnosis of malingering by the clinician?

2.

A. The client demonstrates a psychological need to maintain the "sick role"
B. Further medical examination confirms the impression that the client's symptoms have no physiological basis
C. The client feigns symptoms in order to gain an external reward
D. A clinical presentation characterized by laziness and an "inadequate personality"

3) According to Paul Baltes, individual development across the life span can be described in each of the following ways, EXCEPT

3.

A. multidirectional
B. reversible
C. nonsequential
D. intermittent

4) A social worker has been seeing a mother and daughter for several sessions because of the daughter's repeated defiance of the mother. The mother's responses during most of the sessions have been very child-like. If the social worker were to use transactional analysis with this mother and daughter, he might

4. _____

A. confront the child's fearful behaviors
B. explore mother's feelings toward the child
C. ask the mother and daughter to perform a role reversal
D. encourage the mother to talk to the child as "parent to child"

5)   A clinician decides to use rational-emotive therapy to help a child who   5. _____
is depressed. The FIRST thing the clinician should do to begin the process is

A.   administer the Reynolds Child Depression Scale
B.   interview the child
C.   assess the parents and the child for secondary disturbance
D.   interview the child's parents and teachers

6)   According to the ecological theory of human development and   6. _____
behavior, a "macrosystem" consists of

A.   relations between microsystems or connections between contexts
B.   the patterning of environmental events and transitions over the life course
C.   the attitudes and ideologies of the culture
D.   family, school, peers, and church groups

7)   During a client interview, the social worker tends to phrase his   7. _____
questions so that the client gives "yes" or "no" answers. The overall effect
on the communication process will be that

A.   the social worker will be able to develop a clear chronological picture of
the presenting problem
B.   the client's attitudes and beliefs will eventually be revealed
C.   very little useful information will be elicited
D.   the client will likely become wary and defensive

8)   A client has been forced by the court to attend therapy with a social   8. _____
worker. From a clinical standpoint, it will be MOST important for the social
worker to address

A.   the client's ability to form a relationship with the social worker
B.   the client's ambivalence about treatment
C.   the nature of the client's offense
D.   the latent factors in the client's legal problems

9)   Which of the following does NOT typically characterize a therapy group   9. _____
in its early stages?

A.   Relatively stereotyped and restricted content and communication style
B.   A concern for closeness and intimacy
C.   Giving and seeking advice
D.   Hesitancy and dependence

10)   A 42-year-old client has complained of intermittent abdominal pains,   10. _____
periodic nausea and vomiting, irregular menstrual periods, and periodic weakness
in her limbs. Physical examinations have been normal for the last 3 years. What
diagnosis should the woman receive?

A.   Somatization disorder
B.   Undifferentiated somatoform disorder
C.   Hypochondriasis
D.   Pain disorder associated with psychological factors

11) If the head of a counseling agency hires a consultant to help counselors deal with some particularly difficult cases at the agency, the agency is practicing _____ consultation.

11. _____

A. consultee-centered case
B. consultee-centered administrative
C. program-centered administrative
D. client-centered case

12) In conducting case presentations, it is usually recommended that

12. _____

A. discussion be limited to the case at hand rather than additional problems
B. the practitioner present several cases in one session
C. practitioner dynamics be discussed before case dynamics
D. the practitioner present a specific problem rather than the entire case in context

13) Interventions with Native American clients should generally be focused on

13. _____

A. building on client strengths to solve a particular problem
B. removing environmental obstacles to client success
C. teaching concrete skills to help clients become self-sufficient
D. restoring a balance between physical well-being and spiritual harmony

14) Service eligibility requirements for social service clients are typically _____ in nature.

14. _____

I. Personal
II. Demographic
III. Social
IV. Financial

A. I and IV
B. I, III and IV
C. III and IV
D. I, II, III and IV

15) Client-centered therapy asserts that each of the following therapist attitudes is necessary to effect positive changes in clients, EXCEPT

15. _____

A. genuineness
B. positive regard
C. empathy
D. insightfulness

16) When communicating with the hearing-impaired, a social worker should try to do each of the following, EXCEPT

16. _____

A. speak slowly and clearly
B. reduce background noise
C. face the patient
D. gradually increase the volume of his/her voice

17) Which of the following should generally be done the LATEST in a
crisis intervention with a client who is a battered woman?

17. _____

A.   Asking the client to describe briefly what has just happened
B.   Identifying the client's feelings as asking for a perception check
C.   Making sure the client is now safe and protected
D.   Asking the client if she is taking any medication

18) The area of difference between therapist and client that is likely to be
MOST influential in a therapeutic relationship is

18. _____

A.   gender
B.   socioeconomic status
C.   philosophical orientation
D.   culture

19) After a series of traumatic events at a hospital involving a mother and
her young daughter, who has been experiencing hypoglycemic seizures throughout
the night, the mother, who has been fiercely devoted to her daughter and has remained
at her bedside for more than 24 hours, is inadvertently caught by a nurse in the act of
preparing an insulin injection for the girl. The mother later admitted to giving the insulin
to her daughter. The mother could be said to be suffering from

19. _____

A.   factitious disorder
B.   dissociative disorder
C.   conversion disorder
D.   somatoform disorder

20) Which of the following, if used during the first 3 months of pregnancy,
may cause a cleft palate or other congenital malformation?

20. _____

A.   Alcohol
B.   Tranquilizers
C.   Cocaine
D.   Nicotine

21) Purposes of the Adult Abuse Protocol, an assessment and intervention
guide for the abused adult, include

21. _____

    I.   documenting the violent incident for legal purposes
    II.   alerting the involved hospital staff to provide appropriate clinical care
    III.   provide a formal support network for the client in recovery

A.   I only
B.   I and II
C.   II and III
D.   I, II, and III

22)   Which of the following listening skills is LEAST likely to be used in   22. _____
a client interview that conforms to the behavioral approach?

A.   Open questions
B.   Closed questions
C.   Feedback
D.   Reflection of meaning

23)   The most dangerous side effect associated with phenothiazines is   23. _____

A.   Parkinson-like symptoms
B.   nausea
C.   epileptic seizures
D.   delusional behavior

24)   People who are experiencing anomie are said to adapt in one of five ways. 24. _____
Which of the following is NOT one of these?

A.   Martyrdom
B.   Innovation
C.   Rebellion
D.   Ritualism

25)   Erikson's second stage of psychosocial development, which occurs in   25. _____
late infancy and toddlerhood (1-3 years), is

A.   initiative vs. guilt
B.   trust vs. mistrust
C.   identity vs. identity confusion
D.   autonomy vs. shame and doubt

26)   Questionnaires can be used in preference over other data collection   26. _____
techniques when

        I.   anonymity is important
        II.   budgets are limited
        III. respondents are literate
        IV.   a high response rate is important

A.   I only
B.   I and II
C.   I, II and III
D.   I, II, III and IV

27)   Unlike traditional approaches to psychotherapy, cultural approaches try   27. _____
to understand mental illness from the inside--they attempt to clarify the individual
or group's experience of the illness within the cultural context. In this way, cultural
approaches adopt an _____ perspective.

A.   etiological
B.   endogenous
C.   emic
D.   etic

28) When a person's moral reasoning is controlled by external rewards and punishment, it is said to be

28. _____

A. role-focused
B. preconventional
C. circular
D. preoperational

29) Which of the following individuals if probably the most inappropriate candidate for a long-term interactional therapy group?

29. _____

A. A secretive anorexic-bulimic client
B. A man with a history of sexual promiscuity
C. A client with inadequate ego strength
D. A person who has been convicted of child molestation

30) It is probably most appropriate for a clinician to view professional and formal assessment instruments, such as the Stanford-Binet, Wecshler, and Q-sort as

30. _____

A. providing a full picture of client functions
B. getting in the way of establishing a healthy client/worker relationship
C. ways of confirming impressions
D. uninstrusive means of identifying specific deficits

31) Private-practice clinicians who work full-time calculate that about _____ percent of their gross income goes for operating and overhead expenses if they maintain a full caseload.

31. _____

A. 5–15
B. 20–30
C. 35–45
D. 50–70

32) Which of the following is the BEST example of a secondary prevention program?

32. _____

A. a community education program
B. Head Start
C. Crisis intervention
D. a rehabilitation program

33) Most definitions of "family" tend to focus on the two most significant manifest functions of the family, which are

33. _____

A. production and consumption
B. procreation and the socialization of children
C. production and provision of emotional support
D. procreation and provision of emotional support

34) Within a social services organization, the type of plan that is probably 34. _____
most frequently misunderstood is a(n)

A. mission
B. policy
C. rule
D. budget

35) In the psychodynamic perspective, a "love" that is based on self-doubt 35. _____
will play itself out as _____ love.

A. revengeful
B. sadistic
C. compulsive
D. critical

36) In order to help clients generate additional information about their 36. _____
situations, each of the following is an important skill in interviewing, EXCEPT

A. influencing skills
B. confrontation
C. reflection
D. focusing

37) Which of the following questions is MOST "open" in nature? 37. _____

A. What important things have happened during the week?
B. Where does your daughter live?
C. Could you tell me a little about your family?
D. Do you get along with your mother?

38) Generally, the most strongest predictor of social service utilization by 38. _____
Asian American clients is

A. degree of isolation
B. severity of condition
C. acculturation
D. financial focus of service need

39) The impact of a therapeutic relationship depends on how well a practitioner 39. _____
uses herself or her sensitivity to guide clients in understanding themselves. Which
of the following is NOT an important means of doing this?

A. Exploring thoughts and feelings
B. Listing alternatives
C. Reflecting attitude
D. Modeling behavior

40) For what reason is it sometimes difficult for clinicians to identify depression in young children?   40. _____

A. Depression is often manifested in a variety of symptoms which do not appear to be typical of depression
B. Depression does not exist as a clinical syndrome at that early age
C. Young children do not have sufficient language to describe how they feel
D. Young children do not have the capacity for self-observation

41) Which of the following tasks of remarriage is typically performed FIRST?   41. _____

A. Community remarriage: establishing relationships outside the marriage
B. Parental remarriage: establishing bonds with the children of a partner
C. Legal remarriage: settling financial and other responsibilities toward children and former partners
D. Economic remarriage: becoming interdependent in terms of financial needs and responsibilities

42) Which of the following approaches to social services policymaking tends to recommend a policy based on previous information about the impact of a policy of existing policies, with a projection of continuing future effectiveness?   42. _____

A. Secondary
B. Rational
C. Prescriptive
D. Vertical

43) Most practitioners view _____ as the most important element in bringing about change in clients' lives.   43. _____

A. effective service linkage
B. a strong support network
C. client skill development
D. the therapeutic relationship

44) Individuals with a diagnosis of _____ have a 6-month history of recurrent, intense, sexually arousing fantasies, urges, or behaviors involving touching and rubbing against a nonconsenting person.   44. _____

A. voyeurism
B. exhibitionism
C. frotteurism
D. fetishism

45) A pregnant 14-year-old reports to a social worker complaining about her boyfriend, whom she fights with often because he won't look for work to support her and her child. The girls says she uses cocaine once a week. The social worker should: 45. _____

A. maintain confidentiality and continue therapy
B. consult child protective services, because the girl is a minor and needs protection
C. consult child protective services, because the girl is abusing the fetus
D. call the girl's parents for permission to treat her

46)   Of those who participate in AA, those most likely to benefit are generally   46. _____

A.   members of a lower socioeconomic group
B.   women
C.   older drinkers
D.   heavy drinkers

47)   Which of the following forms of elder maltreatment is LEAST commonly   47. _____
reported?

A.   Physical abuse
B.   Psychological abuse
C.   Financial abuse
D.   Physical neglect

48)   Which of the following is a secondary social work setting?   48. _____

A.   Child welfare agency
B.   Homeless shelter
C.   Alcohol and drug treatment center
D.   Family service agency

49)   In a client interview, a worker may sometimes reflect the client's feelings   49. _____
in a way that is helpful. Which of the following statements about this technique is FALSE?

A.   Reflections in the past tense tend to be more useful than those in the present.
B.   The emotion being reflected should be clearly labeled with a word.
C.   It is often useful to add a contextual word (because, when) to broaden the reflection.
D.   It's important to refer directly to the client in the reflection.

50)   The ideal of human development envisioned by ego psychology is   50. _____

A.   consensus and shared values
B.   individual development across the life course
C.   equality and the absence of alienation and exploitation
D.   mutual self-respect and the absence of labeling

51)   Probably the most frustrating problem encountered by clients in need   51. _____
of services who apply to a public social services agency is the

A.   stigma attached to those who seek services
B.   means-testing process
C.   inability to consider cases individually
D.   size and complexity of the agency's bureaucratic structure

52)   Sample size is social work research has its most direct affect on   52. _____

A.   internal validity
B.   the ability to infer a causal relationship between variables.
C.   experimental control
D.   generalizability

53) According to Piaget, assimilation occurs when individuals 53. _____

A. incorporate new information into their existing knowledge
B. coordinate sensory experiences with physical actions
C. adjust to new information
D. represent the world in words, images and drawings

54) Typically, the relationship between a social worker and a small group 54. _____
differs from that of a social worker and an individual. Which of the following
statements is FALSE regarding the relationship between a worker and a small group?

A. There is greater formality than in a worker/individual relationship.
B. There is an inherent lack of confidentiality.
C. A greater feeling of identification usually exists among clients than in a
worker/individual relationship.
D. Acceptance of others is not mandated to other group members.

55) After the review of a case, an HMO decides to deny further payment for 55. _____
sessions for a social worker's client. The worker believes the client would benefit
from additional therapy. The BEST approach by the worker would be to

A. file a complaint against the HMO
B. consult with the client about his options in this situation
C. comply with the HMO's request, but only if the limits of treatment were
discussed with the client at the beginning of therapy
D. continue to provide therapy to the client without compensation if necessary
until other arrangements can be made

56) The key personality trait in clients who suffer from avoidant personality 56. _____
disorder is

A. an indifference to human contact
B. a distaste for other people
C. a sense of entitlement and lack of empathy
D. a fear of rejection

57) A clinical supervisor who maintains an "open-door" policy with 57. _____
supervisees is MOST likely to encourage the development of

A. unstructured supervision that operates on a crisis basis
B. solution-focused supervision that is focused on client dynamics
C. a proactive style of interaction that locates and attempts to solve problems early
D. a warm peer relationship with practitioners who view the supervisor as an equal

58) In a troubled family it sometimes happens that members project their 58. _____
internal conflicts onto others outside them. These projections are known as

A. triangulations
B. stable coalitions
C. detouring coalitions
D. disengagements

59) The driving force behind a social service agency's resource allocation decisions should be   59. _____

A. the distribution between current vs. long-term debt
B. the available liquid cash resources to cover current debt
C. assets available for collateral for additional debt
D. the mission of the organization

60) The easiest measure of data variability to calculate and understand is   60. _____

A. mean
B. standard deviation
C. range
D. slope

61) The use of "systems" thinking in social work generally involves each of the following advantages, EXCEPT   61. _____

A. it can easily be adapted for the implementation of partial solutions
B. it ensures that a worker will search for more than one way to look at a situation
C. it helps the worker to see the world through the eyes of another
D. it shows that behavior must be understood in the context of a number of factors

62) Sometimes, experiences in another social setting--in which the individual does not have an active role--influence what the individual experiences in an immediate context. This other social setting is described as a(n)   62. _____

A. mesosystem
B. exosystem
C. milieu
D. macrosystem

63) A 30-year old man visits a hospital emergency room complaining of extreme nervousness. When told that he'll have to wait for physician, he becomes irritated and argues with the receptionist, and then paces around the waiting room. An initial physical examination reveals a heart rate of 111 and a blood pressure of 170/110. The man says he's felt extremely nervous, off and on, for several days now. Based on this information only, a practitioner should FIRST investigate the possibility that the man   63. _____

A. is intoxicated with a substance
B. suffers from posttraumatic stress disorder
C. suffers from acute stress disorder
D. has developed generalized anxiety disorder

64) In the stage of a client interview during which the worker and client explore alternatives and confront client incongruities, an important goal is to   64. _____

A. work toward resolution of the client's problem
B. facilitate changes in thoughts, feelings and behaviors in daily life
C. build a working alliance with the client
D. discover the client's ideal world

65) A clinician decides to use Beck's cognitive approach to treat a client with panic disorder. The FIRST goal of intervention would be to for the client to

65. _____

A. see how he misinterprets the meaning of his symptoms
B. identify the antecedents and consequences that are controlling his symptoms
C. understand how the symptoms are controlling different aspects of his life
D. identify the underlying causes of his symptoms

66) Problems associated with labeling in client assessment include

66. _____

    I. masking clients' subjective experience and coping mechanisms
    II. a perceived loss of control by the practitioner
    III. the constraint and trivialization of clients
    IV. an emphasis on what is wrong, rather than what is right

A. I and III
B. I, III and IV
C. II and IV
D. I, II, III and IV

67) The efficiency and effectiveness factors relating to the delivery of social services are evaluated broadly in terms of

67. _____

A. influence
B. summation
C. accountability
D. transactional analysis

68) The functions of an organizational advisory board typically do NOT include

68. _____

A. publicizing agency activities
B. procuring the funds needed to operate the organization
C. evaluating agency services and recommending improvements
D. assisting in determining consumer needs

69) Culturally, the most significantly observed life-cycle transition among African American families is

69. _____

A. birth
B. passing into adulthood
C. marriage
D. death

70) Which of the following is NOT an example of an output goal?

70. _____

A. Reduce the number of alcohol-related incidents of domestic violence by one-third (by 250 incidents)
B. Increase the number of Alcoholics Anonymous and Al-Anon groups in the county by 40% (from 10 to 14) during the coming year.
C. Provide inpatient treatment services to 235 persons with alcohol dependency problems, supplemented with services to their families.
D. Develop a special unit for female alcoholics, increasing service from 40 clients a year to 80 a year.

71) Which of the following interviewing skills generally exerts the greatest   71. _____
amount of influence over client talk?

A.   Interpretation
B.   Open questions
C.   Focusing
D.   Paraphrasing

72) A family reports to a private practitioner out of concern for their young   72. _____
son, who repeatedly urinates in his bed at night and in his clothes during the day.
The parents' attempts to shape the boy's behavior have failed. In order to assign
the boy a diagnosis of enuresis consistent with DSM-IV standards, the practitioner
must establish that

A.   the boy is at least 5 years old
B.   the problem occurs at least once a week
C.   the problem has persisted for at least 6 months
D.   the problem is not related to some external stressor

73) Which of the following processes typically occurs EARLIEST in the   73. _____
therapeutic relationship?

A.   Idealization
B.   Individualization
C.   Identification
D.   Individuation

74) Most developmental psychologists prefer longitudinal research designs to   74. _____
cross-sectional research designs, primarily for the reason that longitudinal designs

A.   use the subjects as their own experimental controls
B.   are much less likely to be influenced by cultural changes that occur over time
C.   offer the advantage of between-subjects comparisons
D.   usually yield results more quickly

75) Most social work professionals agree that paternalism may be justifiable   75. _____
if clients

       I.   are not mentally competent
       II.   might harm themselves seriously
       III.   have repeatedly proven incapable of caring for themselves
       IV.   do not voluntarily consent to a social worker's intervention plan

A.   I and II
B.   III only
C.   I, II, III and IV
D.   None of the above

KEY (CORRECT ANSWERS)

1. C		41. A	
2. C		42. C	
3. D		43. D	
4. D		44. C	
5. D		45. A	
6. C		46. C	
7. C		47. A	
8. B		48. C	
9. B		49. A	
10. B		50. B	
11. D		51. D	
12. A		52. D	
13. D		53. C	
14. B		54. A	
15. D		55. B	
16. D		56. D	
17. A		57. A	
18. D		58. C	
19. A		59. D	
20. B		60. C	
21. B		61. A	
22. D		62. B	
23. A		63. A	
24. A		64. A	
25. D		65. A	
26. C		66. B	
27. C		67. C	
28. B		68. B	
29. A		69. D	
30. C		70. A	
31. B		71. A	
32. C		72. A	
33. B		73. B	
34. B		74. A	
35. C		75. A	
36. C			
37. C			
38. C			
39. B			
40. A			

TEST 2

Directions: Each question or incomplete statement is followed by several suggested answers or completions. Select the one the BEST answers the question or completes the statement. *PRINT THE LETTER OF THE CORRECT ANSWER IN THE SPACE AT THE RIGHT.*

1) The primary purpose of assessment in clinical social work is to ··   1. _____

A. help set appropriate goals and objectives for treatment
B. provide a means of measuring treatment progress and outcome
C. identify an appropriate DSM-IV diagnosis
D. help establish meaningful communication with other providers and insurers

2) An adolescent client, while discussing the murder of her mother by   2. _____
her father, relates the events in a detached, matter-of-fact manner. When emotional blunting of this type occurs in conjunction with _____, a strong likelihood exists that the client is psychotic and in need of psychiatric evaluation.

A. alcohol and/or drug abuse
B. thought disorder
C. unipolar disorder
D. poor self-concept

3) A social worker in private practice receives a phone call from a prospective 3. _____
client who says that she wants to get to know the worker, free of charge, before beginning treatment. The worker should:

A. outline his fee policy for the client
B. see the client
C. tell the client there will be no charge for the session if the worker decides
he cannot work with her
D. inform the client that this isn't possible

4) A clinician in family treatment is dealing with an "undifferentiated ego   4. _____
mass." Which of the following would be an element of the intervention?

D. Forming and join an "emotionally triangle" in the family system in order
to reduce anxiety from within
C. Working individually with the most differentiated family member, because
he/she is most capable of breaking habitual pathological patterns
A. Unbalancing the family's homeostasis by promoting confrontations among
family members
B. Working individually with the least differentiated family member in order to bring
him/her up to the level of the more differentiated family members

5)   A client with a long history of depression visits a clinician for the first time. 5. _____
While the client is hopeful that the clinician can help with his problem, he says he
cannot sign a "non-suicide" contract, and he insists on the additional condition
that the clinician not involuntarily hospitalize him for extreme suicidal thoughts. The
clinician should

A.   inform the client that she cannot make this promise under any circumstances ·
B.   take a medical and social history before deciding to treat this client
C.   try to persuade the client to seek hospitalization for treatment
D.   start a course of antidepressants and check with the client in a few
weeks to see if he's changed his mind

6)   Generally, the thinking today regarding phenotype and genotype is that   6. _____

A.   phenotype reveals certain aspects of genotype
B.   phenotype and genotype have a bidirectional influence on each other
C.   phenotype and genotype have no relation to each other
D.   phenotype does not indicate anything about genotype

7)   Within the context of employee evaluation at a social services agency, the   7. _____
practice of "banding"

A.   is not considered useful because it increases the likelihood that a selection
technique will have an adverse impact
B.   may not reduce adverse impact unless it is combined with a minority
preference component
C.   is considered useful for tracking the success rates of employees who
have been hired using a particular selection technique
D.   is preferable to other techniques because it is more likely to eliminate
problems related to adverse impact

8)   To make acceptance clear to the client in the early stages of building   8. _____
the therapeutic relationship, it's important for the practitioner to

        I.   maintain eye contact with the client
        II.   maintain facial expressions that are consistent with the client's emotions
        III.   keep an appropriate distance away from the client--more than arm's length
        IV.   avoid crossing his/her arms while listening

A.   I only
B.   I and II
C.   I, II and IV
D.   I, II, III and IV

9)   Which of the following clinician roles will generally be LEAST important   9. _____
for a social worker's crisis intervention practice in an emergency room setting?

A.   Educator
B.   Activist
C.   Coordinator
D.   Broker

10)   According to Dane and Simon, one of the predictable problems faced   10. _____
by social workers in secondary practices settings is the "marginality of token
status." This means that

A.   in a given secondary setting, social workers are few and their visibility is
high
B.   social work is devalued as "women's work" in settings that are predominantly
male in composition
C.   there is a discrepancy between the values of the social work profession and the
dominant profession of the organization
D.   a worker who is responsible for developing a helping relationship with the
client in an effort to solve problems must also perform in a role that reinforces the
norms of the organizational setting

11)   Which of the following listening skills is MOST likely to be used in a   11. _____
client interview that conforms to the client-centered approach?

A.   Open questions
B.   Paraphrasing
C.   Closed questions
D.   Interpretation/reframing

12)   Most practitioners, when they begin their careers and begin a relationship   12. _____
with their supervisors, desire help in each of the following areas, EXCEPT

A.   developing skills
B.   finding a specialized niche
C.   fostering self-awareness
D.   applying theory

13)   According to Lewis, the primary difference between a "healthy" and a   13. _____
"faltering" family appears to be in the relationship between

A.   the children
B.   the married couple
C.   the mother and the child/children
D.   the father and the child/children

14)   Which of the following tasks is NOT generally appropriate for   14. _____
paraprofessionals in a social service agency?

A.   Arranging client transportation
B.   Referring clients to appropriate helping professionals
C.   Completing forms requesting services from other agencies
D.   Conducting intake histories

15)   Which of the following term denotes the "pitch" of the voice?   15. _____

A.   Tone
B.   Resonance
C.   Inflection
D.   Volume

16) The "constructivist" model of social work holds that clients' conceptions   16. _____
of reality are a product of

A.   experience
B.   deeds
C.   ideals
D.   language

17) Which of the following is an argument commonly given by social work   17. _____
practitioners AGAINST the use of worker-client contracting in the therapeutic relationship?

A.   Expanded malpractice risks
B.   Greater likelihood of misunderstandings about expectations
C.   Increased likelihood of premature termination
D.   Forces a legal requirement onto the client that damages the status of the
"helping" relationship

18) The symptoms of people with somatization disorder must include the   18. _____
following:

I.   Four pain symptoms in different sites
II.   Two gastrointestinal symptoms without pain
III.   One sexual symptom without pain
IV.   One pseudoneurological symptom without pain

A.   I only
B.   I or II
C.   II, III and IV
D.   I, II, III and IV

19) During a family intervention session, the teen-age daughter is sitting   19. _____
silently in a corner of the room with her arms folded across her chest. To engage
the daughter in the process, clinician using the structural model would

A.   sit next to her and tell her what she's doing is okay and makes perfect sense
B.   direct her to be participate in the agreed-upon intervention
C.   reward and praise her when and if she does speak
D.   ignore her and wait for her to speak when she's ready

20) It is common for Native American or Latino families to ascribe family   20. _____
status to close friends. These friends are said to take on the status of

A.   modified extended members
B.   referents
C.   fictive relatives
D.   de facto kin

21) Advantages to a shared partnership in private social work practice include   21. _____

    I.   Cost savings in office space
    II.   Minimal problems in coverage and consultation
    III.   Increased income- and client-building opportunities
    IV.   Enhanced credibility with other professional groups

A.   I only
B.   I and II
C.   I, III and IV
D.   I, II, III and IV

22) A social worker is interviewing a client who is a recent immigrant   22. _____
from China. In general, the social worker should avoid

A.   attentive body language
B.   sustained eye contact
C.   open-ended questions
D.   verbal tracking

23) Which of the following is NOT a theory of psychoanalysis?   23. _____

A.   The therapist should relate as a real, genuine person.
B.   Mental illness is not an accepted concept.
C.   Insight into problems is insufficient for producing change.
D.   Clients are not responsible for their deviant behaviors.

24) The NASW code states explicitly that a social worker has an ethical   24. _____
duty to provide voluntary public service that benefits society as a whole. Probably
the most appropriate way to do this is to

A.   join and participate in professional organizations or associations
B.   engage in individual advocacy
C.   engage in class advocacy
D.   run for public office

25) Sherman and Wenocur propose six ways for social services workers to   25. _____
resolve their feelings of alienation from the agency. Of these, the most productive is

A.   withdrawal
B.   functional non-capitulation
C.   niche-finding
D.   capitulation

26) In the psychodynamic perspective, "falling in love" is best described as   26. _____

A.   the unrealistic search for the perfect partner
B.   a sign that inner needs are finally being met
C.   an idealization of the sexual drive
D.   an irrational process

27)   Which of the following relationships is an example of a purchase of   27. _____
service agreement?

A.   A child protective services agency contracts with a family services agency to
provide counseling to children who have suffered abuse or neglect.
B.   A psychotherapist refers a client to a general assistance agency for help with
financial management.
C.   A family services agency hires the legal advisors of the local hospital to help
with a malpractice suit.
D.   A general assistance client applies for and is given food stamps to supplement
his income

28)   According to Freud, which of the following defense mechanisms is   28. _____
ALWAYS involved in neurotic behavior?

A.   sublimation
B.   regression
C.   anger
D.   repression

29)   In the transactional view of human behavior,   29. _____

A.   it is believed that human potential is limitless
B.   people are motivated primarily by the potential for profit
C.   the primary issue is the tension between individual and collective well-being
D.   people are seen as individual systems, separate from their social context

30)   The client of a private practitioner complains of frequent periods of   30. _____
dizziness during which he experiences several unsettling feelings: he feels completely
separate from his mind and body, as if he's floating and watching himself from
above. The client says that during these episodes he sometimes wonders whether
he's a real person or some machine that's programmed by someone else.   The client
is aware that the feelings are a product of his mind, but he can't control them, though
he has been keeping them to himself and not telling family or friends about them.
The most appropriate diagnosis for this client is

A.   dementia, not otherwise specified
B.   depersonalization disorder
C.   delusional disorder
D.   schizophreniform disorder

31)   During an initial interview, a client tells the social worker that he is gay 31. _____
and has AIDS. For the worker and this client to have an effective long-term
therapeutic relationship, it is most important for the worker to be:

A.   gay
B.   non-homophobic
D.   ready to refer the client out
C.   comfortable dealing with issues of sexuality and safe sex

32) Which of the following statements is TRUE?   32. _____

A.   There is no consistent correlation between ethnic, racial, or socioeconomic status and the likelihood of child abuse or neglect.
B.   Mothers are more likely to be implicated in cases of abuse and neglect than fathers.
C.   In general, the likelihood that a child will experience neglect decreases with age.
D.   Boys are twice as likely as girls to experience abuse or neglect.

33) As a social worker leads a therapy group, a client offers constructive   33. _____
feedback to another client in the group, but the feedback is offered in clear
irritation and agitation. The rest of the group becomes angry at the first client.
The social worker should:

A.   point out what the first client did well, and then offer constructive criticism
B.   see the first client in an individual session to give him feedback on his performance
C.   ask the group to point out what the first client has done wrong
D.   focus on the needs of the client who has just received negative feedback

34) A practitioner in private practice is visited by a mother and her, an   34. _____
exceptionally bright 11-year-old who is not at all liked by his peers. Their
dislike has become so strong that they continually tease and taunt the boy,
and he has complained bitterly to his mother. Probably the most useful means
of assessment in this situation would be for the practitioner to

A.   arrange situations in which the boy's behavior around other children can be observed
B.   begin a course of insight-oriented treatment
C.   gently question the boy about what he believes might be causing the problem
D.   set up a role-playing exercise in which the boy assumes the role of one of his classmates

35) In removing personal barriers to achievement for clients of color,   35. _____
interventions should be aimed at

A.   distributing resources through information/education
B.   actively encouraging family involvement
C.   recognizing and affirming client system strengths
D.   improving educational/vocational opportunities through greater teacher/employer awareness of diversity, history and customs

36) Which of the following is NOT a type of behavioral intervention?   36. _____

A.   Systematic desensitization
B.   Assertiveness training
C.   Script analysis
D.   Contingency contracting

37) In couples therapy, it is most important for the social worker to   37. _____

A.   establish rapport with each partner
B.   maintain confidentiality
C.   cut through the denial
D.   teach communication skills

38) A clinician collects different kinds of data--for example, interviews and observations--which may include both qualitative and quantitative data, for the purpose of studying the same research question. This is an example of

    38. _____

A.   triangulation
B.   cross-classification
C.   rival hypotheses
D.   validation

39) Ivan Nye and his associates, applying the social exchange theory to family life, concluded that behavioral choices made by family members follow a specific, rank-order pattern, beginning with choices from alternatives

    39. _____

A.   from which they anticipate the fewest costs
B.   that provide better immediate outcomes
C.   from which they expect the most profit
D.   that promise better long-term outcomes

40) Of the types of adolescents listed below, psychodynamic interventions will probably be MOST useful for those

    40. _____

A.   who are addicted and in denial
B.   with oppositional/conduct disorder
C.   who are clinically depressed
D.   with ADHD

41) A family has been seeing a social worker for almost one year, after receiving a court referral--their 15-year-old son was found guilty of sexually molesting their 7-year-old daughter. The son has been in foster care for the last year and has been receiving individual and group therapy. In one month, he is due to begin visitations at home. The social worker should

    41. _____

A.   reiterate to the family what they've learned about the "cycle of incest"
B.   include the son in a family therapy session during his first visitation
C.   contact the son's individual and group therapists for copies of their opinions as to his readiness for family therapy, and coordinate treatment with them
D.   review the family's plans for what will take place in terms of the son's interactions with his sister during initial visitations

42) Which of the following question stems is particularly useful to social workers in client interviews, because it is simultaneously open and closed?

    42. _____

A.   What
B.   Could
C.   Is
D.   How

43)   Which of the following statements is NOT characteristic of ego   43. _____
psychology?

A.   The social environment shapes the personality
B.   Problems are almost exclusively the function of deficits in coping capacity
C.   The ego mediates between the individual and the environment
D.   The ego is the part of the personality that allows for successful adaptation to the
environment.

44)   Questioning is one of the most important means for supervisors to help   44. _____
practitioners reflect on their own work. Which of the following is a guideline to
for a supervisor to use in questioning an practitioner?

A.   When the supervisor wonders whether the practitioner has adequate
knowledge of the case or diagnosis, to make treatment decision, the supervisor
should move from specific to general questions.
B.   Beginning questions should be specific in nature and answered specifically.
C.   When general supervisory questions result in answers that reveal thorough knowledge
of the case, the supervisor can move to questions related to treatment and intervention
strategies.
D.   Questions related to treatment strategies and techniques should be more specific than
questions related to diagnostic understanding.

45)   In applying the ethical concept of client self-determination, a social   45. _____
worker upholds:

A.   the importance of helping clients make healthy choices and decisions
B.   the right and need of clients to make their own choices and decisions
C.   the importance of helping clients achieve their fullest potential
D.   the right of clients to seek help in making choices and decisions

46)   According to Bowen, families deal with anxiety and tension in one of   46. _____
four ways. Which of the following is NOT one of these?

A.   Increased emotional distance between spouses
B.   Increased emotional distance between siblings
C.   Physical or emotional dysfunction in a spouse
D.   Impairment in a child

47)   Which of the following offers the BEST example of a double-bind   47. _____
paradox?

A.   A father who masks hostility with a too-loving attitude
B.   An authoritarian mother
C.   A passive mother and a hostile son
D.   An aggressive mother and a timid son

48)   Which of the following is a phenotypical definition of gender?   48. _____

A.   Genital gender
B.   Hormonal gender
C.   Organal gender
D.   Chromosomal gender

49) Which of the following approaches to social services policymaking is   49. _____
designed to meet a long-term need, such as education?

A. Formative
B. Residual
C. External
D. Investment

50) In the early stages of a therapeutic relationship, the practitioner brings   50. _____
the focus of discussions onto the client herself, and affirming her willingness
and ability to bring about necessary change. Probably the next stage for this
relationship will be to

A. connect various elements of current client problems to patterns of their life
experience
B. client internalization of appropriate goals, attitudes and behaviors
C. creating structures and patterns of learning and awareness
D. recognizing and admiring client abilities to grow independent and create
something valuable

51) Which of the following ethnic groups are generally LEAST likely to   51. _____
the placement of older relations into a nursing home?

A. Latino
B. Chinese-American
C. African-American
D. Jewish-American

52) The general consensus among clinical social workers and psychologists   52. _____
is that a person in crisis is characterized by each of the following, EXCEPT

A. appearing unable to modify or lessen the impact of stressful events with
traditional coping methods
B. experiencing a serious loss of function
C. experiencing increased fear, tension and/or confusion
D. exhibiting a high level of subjective discomfort

53) Within a social services organization, zero-based budgeting   53. _____

I. requires that a program start from scratch
II. requires that a program justify each dollar requested
III. is calculated annually
IV. rolls unused funds into the next program

A. I only
B. I and II
C. I, II and III
D. I, II, III and IV

54)   In the theoretical construct of self psychology, drives are seen as more   54. _____
_____ than in the Freudian approach.

A.   social
B.   libidinal
C.   aggressive
D.   instinctual

55)   Among social work clinicians, one of the major problems with the   55. _____
concept of acceptance in a therapeutic relationship is that

A.   clinicians often become overinvolved and make the client's needs into
their own
B.   the duration of such relationships usually doesn't allow for
acceptance
C.   clinicians often confuse it with liking the person or approving of
client behaviors
D.   clients often don't care whether they are accepted or not as long as
their problem is solved

56)   During the assessment phase of treatment for the family of a child with   56. _____
conduct disorder, the practitioner should focus attention on each of the following,
EXCEPT

A.   information about cognitive/emotional reactions to the presenting problem
B.   solutions already attempted by the family
C.   the reasons why people react to the presenting problem in the ways that they do
D.   family myths

57)   Which of the following is NOT a recent professional trend that has   57. _____
supported the need for clinical supervision of practitioners?

A.   Changes in professional standards
B.   Resurgence of clinical practice
C.   Complex external controls on practice structure
D.   Decreasing role of social work in mental illness treatment

58)   During an initial interview session with a family, the social worker   58. _____
observes that family therapist notices that whenever the mother talks, the
father and son contradict what she says and criticize her. The father and son's
behavior is best described as:

A.   triangulation
B.   scapegoating
C.   a coalition
D.   positive feedback

59)   In making her assessment of the occurrence of depression in a   59. _____
community, a practitioner begins to worry that the problem is not as serious
as has been suggested by several recent well-publicized events. The practitioner
should

A.   rely on clients' definitions of their individual problems
B.   put her theories and preconceptions on hold until she has gathered more
information
C.   engage in self-exploration to heighten sensitivity to misplaced assumptions
and expectations
D.   check statistical data and data on non-occurrence

60)   In order to be accurate, a paraphrase of a client's statements must   60. _____
contain certain elements. Which of the following is NOT necessarily one of these?

A.   A succinct summary of what the client said, in the same order it was said
B.   A brief signal at the end of the paraphrase that asks whether it is accurate
C.   A sentence stem using some aspect of the client's mode of receiving information
D.   The key words and constructs used by the client to describe the situation or person.

61)   Which of the following approaches to social services policymaking   61. _____
focuses on a specific need, such as food stamps?

A.   Institutional
B.   Consumption
C.   Coalition
D.   Prescriptive

62)   By far, the most readily available data in assessment are the anecdotal data   62. _____
provided in interviews with the client. This type of information carries the risk of

A.   masking the client's perceptions of his own experience
B.   a focus on client deficits
C.   "pigeon-holing" the client in the worker's eyes into a neat category of presenting
problem
D.   worker counter-transference

63)   The Rational Decision-Making Model is used by some social service   63. _____
administrators in program evaluation and design. In the first stage of the model,
problem formulation, administrators

        I.   identify stakeholders in the evaluation
        II.   specify the relationship between the evaluation and the program
        III.   specify types of data to be collected
        IV.   clarify the objectives of the evaluation

A.   I and II
B.   I and IV
C.   II, III and IV
D.   I, II, III and IV

64)   In the conduct of life span research, effects that are due to a subject's time   64. _____
of birth, but which are unrelated to age, are known as

A.   age-graded influences
B.   chronosystems
C.   normative life events
D.   cohort effects

65)   A practitioner incrementally adds specific treatment components to a   65. _____
client's treatment package, in order to monitor their collective impact. This
type of intervention is known as a _____ treatment strategy.

A.   dismantling
B.   dichotomous
C.   constructive
D.   parametric

66)   One of the clinician's tasks in crisis intervention is to restore a client's   66. _____
cognitive functioning. In developing cognitive mastery, the client must FIRST

A.   restructure, rebuild, and replace irrational beliefs with new, realistic cognitions
B.   obtain a realistic understanding of what happened and what led to the crisis
C.   explore feelings and emotions surrounding the incident
D.   understand the specific meaning the event has for him or her

67)   Which of the following is NOT a type of "in-kind" social service program?   67. _____

A.   Food stamps
B.   Public housing
C.   General assistance
D.   Medical assistance

68)   Which of the following statements about child abuse/maltreatment   68. _____
is FALSE?

A.   It occurs in nearly half of all families.
B.   It is usually mild to moderate in severity.
C.   It is a diverse condition.
D.   It is only partially caused by parental personality characteristics.

69)   In social work practice, the corrective experience that allows clients to   69. _____
experience themselves differently, and thereafter make changes, begins as a function of

A.   the client's willingness to change
B.   how much the client is able to trust the practitioner to help him make the
right decisions about how to change
C.   the degree to which the practitioner can establish an empathic understanding of the
client and his situation
D.   the degree to which the practitioner can establish a sense of urgency for change

70)   During an initial interview with a divorced 37-year-old man, the client   70. _____
reports that he suspects his ex-wife, who is the custodial parent of their daughter,
of abusing her. The MOST appropriate response for the worker would be to

A.   ask the client whether he has reported the abuse
B.   explore the factors that have led the client to believe this
C.   begin therapy cautiously, mindful of the possibility that the client may
be using this allegation to obtain custody of his daughter
D.   report child abuse in accord with a social worker's legal mandate to make
a suspected child abuse report whenever he or she hears about possible child abuse

71)   Studies comparing the personalities of lesbian and heterosexual females   71. _____
have found that

A.   lesbian women are less defensive than heterosexual women
B.   lesbian women are higher in neuroticism than heterosexual women
C.   lesbian women and heterosexual women are about equally well-adjusted
D.   lesbian women are less confident than heterosexual women

72)   Which of the following is a significant benefit associated with the   72. _____
psychoanalytical model of intervention?

A.   easily operationalized concepts
B.   attention to personality development across the entire human life span
C.   clear recognition of the subconscious in psychological functioning
D.   pan-cultural theoretical base

73)   Which of the following investigative strategies is designed to   73. _____
achieve a precise determination of a behavior's causes?

A.   Random assignment
B.   Correlational
C.   Longitudinal
D.   Experimental

74)   As part of an evaluation program, a social worker records the number of   74. _____
times a child replies to a specific parental request. The observational method used
here is

A.   time sampling
B.   recording latency
C.   counting discriminated operants
D.   frequency count

75)   Which of the following questions or statements is MOST likely to be used   75. _____
during a client interview by a social worker using the Rogerian model?

A.   On the other hand, you see your ideal self as someone who can excel at
managing both a career and a family.
B.   You say you often act awkwardly in social situations, and you'd like to
develop some social skills?
C.   I think you've described your short-term and long-term goals pretty clearly.
D.   I'm beginning to see the difference here between your present situation and
your desired outcome.

KEY (CORRECT ANSWERS)

1.	A	41.	C
2.	B	42.	B
3.	A	43.	B
4.	C	44.	C
5.	A	45.	B
6.	D	46.	B
7.	B	47.	A
8.	C	48.	A
9.	B	49.	D
10.	A	50.	C
11.	B	51.	B
12.	B	52.	B
13.	B	53.	B
14.	B	54.	A
15.	C	55.	C
16.	D	56.	C
17.	D	57.	D
18.	D	58.	C
19.	A	59.	D
20.	C	60.	A
21.	D	61.	B
22.	B	62.	D
23.	D	63.	B
24.	C	64.	D
25.	B	65.	C
26.	D	66.	B
27.	A	67.	C
28.	D	68.	A
29.	C	69.	C
30.	B	70.	B
31.	B	71.	C
32.	B	72.	C
33.	A	73.	D
34.	A	74.	C
35.	C	75.	A
36.	C		
37.	D		
38.	A		
39.	C		
40.	C		

EXAMINATION SECTION

Directions: Each question or incomplete statement is followed by several suggested answers or completions. Select the one the BEST answers the question or completes the statement. *PRINT THE LETTER OF THE CORRECT ANSWER IN THE SPACE AT THE RIGHT.*

1) At the outset of treatment, a client tells the social worker that she must promise never to involuntarily hospitalize her, no matter how depressed or suicidal she may seem. In formulating a response to this request, the social worker should use the underlying ethical principle of   1. _____

A. the need to do whatever is necessary to maintain a therapeutic relationship with a client
B. never making a promise that is in conflict with legal and ethical requirements
C. the client's right to self-determination
D. the understanding that the client has legitimate, defensible reasons for making this request

2) For a Gestalt therapist, a primary goal of treatment is to help the client   2. _____

A. integrate the present with his/her past and future
B. develop a "success identity"
C. integrate the functioning of his/her mind and body
D. incorporate the external into the internal

3) What is the term for a social system that is part of a larger system and made up of several smaller systems?   3. _____

A. Focal system
B. Schema
C. Holon
D. Gemeinschaft

4) The most commonly occurring psychological disorders are _____ disorders.   4. _____

A. Dissociative
B. Psychosexual
C. Mood
D. Somatoform

5) In the early stages of problem-solving communication training with a family, the practitioner should FIRST assess   5. _____

A. family cognitions about communication/arguments
B. the history of the problem
C. family assets
D. specific skill deficits

6) An intern at an agency for the chronically mentally ill meets with a 24-year-old client who has been referred by his family doctor. The primary basis for this referral is the client's isolation from peers and general lack of social skills. In many ways, the client reminds the intern of the quiet, studious friends she made in graduate school, who had very little time to socialize because of studies and part-time jobs. The client tells the intern he doesn't think he belongs in this place, and she silently agrees, though her supervisor and more experienced workers seem to believe that this is the right place for him. In her assessment of this client's situation, the intern has relied on the _____ heuristic.

6. _____

A. theoretical
B. schematic
C. availability
D. representativeness

7) Which of the following types of feminism proposes that men and women have different values due to the structure of sex and gender roles in society?

7. _____

A. socialist
B. reactionary
C. radical
D. liberal

8) The most significant problem with establishing "comparable worth" at an agency is that

8. _____

A. males and females may use different strategies to reach the same decision or solution
B. the job evaluation techniques themselves may be gender-biased
C. job evaluation techniques are not as useful for very complex jobs
D. it is difficult to compare achievement across different domains

9) A social worker decides that solution-focused therapy is the most appropriate approach for a family that has come to see her about financial problems. The social worker's FIRST intervention would be to

9. _____

A. discuss time constraints and make sure the family knows the intervention will be brief
B. get a clear picture of how the system functions
C. get a history of the origins of the symptoms
D. discuss how things would be for the family if the problem was already solved

10) Social service agencies, in attempting to make a certain program more efficient and useful, may sometimes get lost in pursuing a prescribed means of service delivery at the expense of accomplishing program goals. This is known as

10. _____

A. output loss
B. goal displacement
C. bounded rationality
D. organizational shaping

11) According to Elkind, the most significant descriptor of adolescent thought is

    11. _____

A. concrete
B. irrational
C. egocentric
D. moralistic

12) In a program evaluation, which type of data is concerned primarily with whether or not the program goals are being met?

    12. _____

A. throughput
B. process
C. product
D. input

13) Which of the following problems or disorders is LEAST likely to be changed through psychotherapy?

    13. _____

A. Anorexia nervosa
B. Conduct disorder
C. Antisocial personality disorder
D. Compulsive behavior

14) The record-keeping requirements at a typical social services agency require the completion of a review treatment plan at an interval no longer than

    14. _____

A. after every client contact
B. weekly
C. every 30 days
D. every 90 days

15) For social workers, it is usually most appropriate to view a woman's separation from an abusive husband as

    15. _____

A. a series of losses which initiates a mourning process
B. a solution that must be accomplished as quickly as possible
C. a partial process at best if children are involved
D. the best of all possible solutions to the problem of domestic abuse

16) Formative policy research at social services agencies

    16. _____

A. is usually conducted in response to legislative mandates
B. focuses on policy development rather than on its impact on clients and agencies
C. identifies social policy as the independent variable
D. is based entirely on output goals

17) Abusive families are most often characterized by

    17. _____

A. openness and affection
B. rigid boundaries and clear roles
C. a strong parental subsystem
D. denial and enmeshed boundaries

18)   The principal assessment tool for clinicians working from the   18. _____
intergenerational perspective on the family is the

A.   life cycle matrix
B.   social history
C.   genogram
D.   ecomap

19)   The "output goals" of a social service program are MOST likely to include   19. _____

A.   specified ratings of services by clients on a standardized scale
B.   observable effects on a given community or clientele
C.   the number of units of service provided
D.   the number of clients served

20)   A 35-year-old client, a high school teacher, reports to a practitioner   20. _____
at an outpatient clinic and reports the following incident: he, a high school
teacher, was in the middle of a lesson during a class period that had been
particularly difficult for him over the past several months, because the class
was large and often noisy. During the middle of today's lesson, the client
suddenly began to sweat profusely and his heart started to race. He continued
with the lesson but soon felt dizzy and fearful that he was about to die. The feeling
was so overwhelming that he had to leave the class unattended and retreat to the
teacher's lounge, where he was found sitting alone and trembling. The client's
physician has found no evidence of medical problems. The most likely DSM-IV
diagnosis for this client would be

A.   panic disorder
B.   posttraumatic stress disorder
C.   dissociative disorder
D.   social phobia

21)   Which of the following statements reveals a client with a formal-operational 21. _____
emotional orientation?

A.   I'm so sad right now that my stomach hurts. I haven't eaten all day.
B.   I suppose there are two different ways of looking at this. On one hand, these
arguments are really painful, but I know I have to set limits for my son and it's part of my role
as a parent. I know he needs to find his own space, but his decisions are sometimes
questionable.
C.   I feel great about the new relationship I'm in. I think I've met the perfect man.
D.   As I think about it, I feel bad because it seems as if we've been arguing a lot lately.
It's almost a ritual--every time I get ready to leave the house, an argument starts.

22)   The purpose of the mental status examination in psychotherapy is   22. _____

A.   personality testing
B.   to make a diagnosis
C.   reality testing
D.   to determine the severity of psychotic symptoms

23) Which of the following interviewing skills is most useful for discovering   23. _____
the deeply held thoughts and feelings underlying the client's experience?

A.   Confrontation
B.   Open-ended questioning
C.   Focusing
D.   Reflection of meaning

24) A client who has a history of hypomanic and major depressive episodes   24. _____
would have a diagnosis of

A.   Hypomanic disorder
B.   Cyclothymic disorder
C.   Bipolar I disorder
D.   Bipolar II disorder

25) Which of the following theoretical frameworks establishes equity   25. _____
and distributive justice as its ideal ends of development

A.   Behavioral/social exchange
B.   Ego psychology
C.   Symbolic interactionism
D.   Structural functionalism

26) A "Theory X" manager in an organization is likely to   26. _____

A.   adopt a team approach to problem-solving
B.   use tangible rewards and sanctions to shape employee behavior
C.   work to set up and maintain a work environment that promotes
growth and creativity
D.   assume that subordinates want to work toward organization goal
attainment

27) Which of the following is generally NOT recommended as part of an   27. _____
intervention with a Native American client who follows older traditions?

A.   Serving food
B.   Emphasizing the past
C.   Giving gifts
D.   Including friends and family

28) The process of transforming a piece of legislation into a specific   28. _____
program or policy, by means of identifying specific guidelines and operating
procedures to be used in administering the program, is known as

A.   rationalization
B.   promulgation
C.   consignment
D.   confederation

29) Which of the following is NOT an ego-defense mechanism?   29. _____

A. Regression
B. Reality testing
C. Displacement
D. Sublimation

30) Which of the following is probably the MOST appropriate candidate   30. _____
for an intensive, heterogeneous outpatient therapy group?

A. A paranoid person
B. A person with bipolar II disorder
C. An alcoholic or drug addict
D. A person with brain damage

31) In removing intracultural barriers to achievement for clients of color,   31. _____
interventions should be aimed at

A. active encouragement of family involvement
B. recognition and affirmation of client system strengths
C. changes in institutional policies, practices, and administration
D. improved educational/vocational opportunities through greater teacher/employer
awareness of diversity, history and customs

32) Which of the following is a means-tested program?   32. _____

A. Medicare
B. Social Security
C. Public education
D. Police protection

33) One of the greatest risks associated with too little self-disclosure in the   33. _____
group therapy process is

A. severely limited reality testing
B. low group cohesiveness
C. yielding an inappropriate amount of member control
D. severe dependence

34) In behavioral therapy, the systematic desensitization process, usually   34. _____
performed by disassociating a neutral stimulus from a situation that has created fear
or anxiety, is also known as

A. extinction
B. aversion therapy
C. overcorrection
D. counterconditioning

35) The primary function of reflecting feelings during a client interview is to   35. _____

A. help the client sort out mixed or ambivalent feelings
B. grounding the worker and client in concrete experience
C. bring out additional details of the client's emotional world
D. make implicit, sometimes hidden emotions clear to the client

36) Which of the following is NOT a privileged relationship during the prosecution of child abuse?

36. _____

A. Priest-confessor
B. Lawyer-client
C. Psychotherapist-patient
D. Physician-patient

37) According to ego psychology, the ego

37. _____

A. mediates between erotic energies and superego constraints
B. is a drive for pleasure
C. imposes a set of rules to control unbridled pleasure-seeking
D. offers ideals for the individual to strive for

38) Which of the following statements reveals a discrepancy that is external to the speaker?

38. _____

A. I don't mind talking about that at all.
B. I wanted to go to business school, but my grades weren't good enough.
C. My mother is a saint, but she doesn't respect me.
D. This is a nice office. It's too bad it's in this neighborhood.

39) During an intake interview for a woman who has committed a violent crime, the clinician notes that whenever the woman talks of the act she does so without any emotion--anger, shame, guilt, or sadness--whatsoever. From the psychoanalytic perspective, the woman is using the defense mechanism of

39. _____

A. isolation
B. fantasy formation
C. repression
D. rationalization

40) A humanist, looking at an individual's misbehavior, would conclude that a person who acts badly is

40. _____

A. suffering from a kind of illness
B. experiencing a detachment from her moral compass
C. willfully disregarding the norms which characterize her community
D. reacting to the deprivation of her basic needs

41) Clinicians in private practice are generally paid for

41. _____

    I. direct services to clients
    II. number of hours on the job
    III. indirect services

A. I only
B. I and II
C. II only
D. I, II and III

42)   A clinician is meeting with a transactional group for the first time and works intensely at studying the members and their transactions. In the early stages of work with this group, the clinician's greatest challenge is likely to be

42. _____

A.   defusing conflict between members
B.   identifying the self-talk or cognitions that lie behind a transaction
C.   heading off the tendency toward subgroupings
D.   determining which ego state a transaction comes from

43)   A social worker has been seeing a client for several months and has developed a good working relationship. The client loses her job and cannot afford to pay for therapy. Under the social worker's professional code and value system, the BEST option in this case would be to

43. _____

A.   refer the client to low-cost therapy from another provider
B.   allow the client to divert payments until she gets another job
C.   provide the therapy free of charge until the client can find employment
D.   reduce the fee for this client and/or offer her shorter sessions

44)   "Acceptance" in the therapeutic relationship mean that the practitioner

44. _____

I.   separates the client from her behavior
II.   indicates approval of the client's behavior
III.   expresses sympathy for the client
IV.   demonstrates tolerance for client's behavior

A.   I only
B.   I and II
C.   II, III and IV
D.   I, II, III and IV

45)   According to Papernow, most people first enter a stepfamily with

45. _____

A.   a clear awareness of the reality of their situation
B.   a growing sense of realistic intimacy with new family members
C.   the fantasy that they will rescue the new partner and any children from the deficiencies of a previous marriage
D.   a feeling of resentment toward new family members who place new demands on their time, money, and other resources

46)   An ideal therapeutic relationship in social work is one that

46. _____

A.   connects the client with the proper support services
B.   allows and helps the client's capacity to work out his own issues
C.   is an ongoing source of support
D.   the client can rely upon as a problem-solving tool

47)   Which of the following is NOT characteristic of a clinician who is conducting reality therapy with a client?

47. _____

A.   Viewing mental illness labels as destructive
B.   Focusing on behavior rather than feelings
C.   Discouraging value judgements
D.   Not offering sympathy

48) In general, a DSM-IV diagnosis of a specific disorder includes a criterion of

48. _____

A. no medical involvement
B. a clinically significant impairment or distress in a social or occupational area
C. an identifiable etiology
D. distress that has exceeded a period of 8 weeks

49) A client interview is interrupted by a long silence that makes the social worker uncomfortable. The FIRST thing the social worker should do is

49. _____

A. inform the client that of his/her (the worker's) discomfort and observe the client's reaction
B. restate the last words spoken by the client
C. say, "I wonder why you're so quiet"
D. study the client to see if he/she appears comfortable with the silence

50) A social worker is seeing a Latino family that immigrated to the United States several years ago. The social worker is not Latino. The family often arrive late for their sessions, causing some scheduling problems--and mild annoyance--for the social worker. The best way for the social worker to handle this would be to

50. _____

A. be aware that time may be perceived differently in their culture and invite them to discuss what being late means to them
B. understand that being late is probably an expression of cultural resistance to disclosing family issues
C. be aware that time may be perceived differently in their culture, and take a more flexible approach to beginning scheduled sessions
D. consider referring the family to a Hispanic therapist

51) The foundation of clinical supervisory techniques--and the focus of supervision--is/are typically

51. _____

A. case material
B. educational assessment
C. long-term practitioner development goals
D. practitioner attitudes and values

52) A practitioner grew up as the oldest child of alcoholic parents, and was often placed in the role of parent to his three younger siblings. In order to establish solid therapeutic relationships with his clients, the most important challenge this practitioner will probably face is

52. _____

A. being able to trust that clients have the capacity to work through their problems
B. being able to see clearly the problems faced by alcoholic clients
C. the risk that he will impose an undue level of responsibility on clients early in the intervention process
D. a lack of faith in his ability to help clients change

53)   A married couple and their two teenage sons see a clinician for the first time for help with what they view as an unhealthy spirit of competition between the two boys. The clinician observes the family's interactions and characterizes them as high-functioning and relatively flexible. Which of the following models of intervention is probably MOST appropriate for this family?

A.   Structural-functional
B.   Strategic
C.   Experiential
D.   Solution-focused

53. _____

54)   According to the lifespan perspective of human development and behavior, development is NOT

A.   contextual
B.   historically embedded
C.   unidirectional
D.   lifelong

54. _____

55)   The sole motivation for a client's feigning illness in factitious disorder is to

A.   obtain prescription drugs
B.   draw attention away from his/her psychological problems
C.   assume a sick role.
D.   escape material and everyday responsibilities

55. _____

56)   In school, an 8-year-old boy has considerably impaired social interactions with other children, along with severely impaired language skills. The boy also pulls at his hair constantly, sometimes leaving ragged bald patches, and often bites himself, leaving wounds and scars that his parents have made the primary concern for treatment. Appropriate diagnoses for this boy include

I.   Asperger's disorder
II.   Stereotypic movement disorder
III.   Autism
IV.   Mental retardation

A.   I and II
B.   II and III
C.   III only
D.   IV only

56. _____

57)   In order to ensure a margin of error no greater than 5%, what is the size of the sample required to represent a population of 10,000?

A.   108
B.   370
C.   1235
D.   9,500

57. _____

58)   Social learning theory recognizes each of the following as a key factor in human development, EXCEPT

58. _____

A.   cognition
B.   heredity
C.   behavior
D.   environment

59)   According to Annon, clients in sex therapy need interventions at very specific levels. The first of these levels is

59. _____

A.   specific suggestions
B.   intensive therapy
C.   limited information
D.   permission

60)   Which of the following is named as the etiological agent for adjustment disorder?

60. _____

A.   Depressed mood
B.   Stress
C.   Sudden trauma
D.   Organic chemistry imbalance

61)   Social workers generally observe several distinct characteristics in the life cycle of poor African-American families. Which of the following is NOT one of these?

61. _____

A.   Households that are frequently female-headed and isolated from the community
B.   A scarceness of resources that compels a reliance on government institutions
C.   A truncated life cycle with less time to resolve developmental tasks
D.   A life cycle punctuated by numerous unpredictable life events

62)   A 50-year-old client has been significantly depressed for more than a year. For the past two months, the client has been convinced that he has developed lung cancer. The most appropriate DSM-IV diagnosis for the client would be

62. _____

A.   conversion disorder
B.   major depressive episode
C.   somatoform disorder, not otherwise specified
D.   hypochondriasis

63)   Persuasive arguments for flexible-rate fee schedules include

63. _____

I.   Services more accessible to disadvantaged clients
II.   Endorsements of insurers and other third-party organizations
III.   No means testing
IV.   Consistency with consumer protection laws

A.   I only
B.   I and III
C.   I, II and IV
D.   I, II, III and IV

64) The psychoanalytical perspective views _____ as the most powerful and pervasive defense mechanism.   64. _____

A. projection
B. rationalization
C. repression
D. denial

65) Which of the following approaches to client interviewing is MOST likely to make use of interpretation or reframing?   65. _____

A. Psychodynamic
B. Solution-focused
C. Client-centered
D. Behavioral

66) When a clinician is on a provider panel for a managed health care company, he or she: 66. _____

A. is guaranteed a certain number of referrals from this company per year.
B. has met the qualifications for company, and has no guarantee of referrals.
C. agree to see any referral within your specialty.
D. will receive a full fee from the company when he/she sees a client

67) When a therapeutic relationship is functioning on the cognitive level, the therapist will probably engage in each of the following processes, EXCEPT   67. _____

A. highlighting inconsistencies
B. reassuring
C. reframing
D. asking key questions

68) Several days after losing her job, a woman becomes so depressed that she is unable to get out of bed until well into the afternoon, and rarely leaves her home. By the time she reports to a practitioner for treatment, she has been depressed and had trouble sleeping for about 4 months. The most appropriate DSM-IV diagnosis for this client is   68. _____

A. major depressive episode
B. dysthmic disorder
C. adjustment disorder with depressed mood
D. depressive disorder, not otherwise specified

69) The NASW code's prohibition of dual relationships is most likely to be challenged by social workers who   69. _____

A. are part of an interdisciplinary team
B. live and work in rural areas
C. are involved in direct practice
D. perform supervisory functions

70) Many practitioners make use of informal assessment instruments such as self-reporting questionnaires, indexes, and profiles. The main risk associated with these instruments as assessment tools is that they   70. _____

A. often put the client on the defensive
B. may place too much emphasis on relatively unimportant details
C. suggest that the practitioner may be lazy or incompetent
D. often provoke client dissembling

71) The term "active listening" mostly refers to a person's ability to   71. _____

A. indicate with numerous physical cues that he/she is listening
B. take an active role in determining which information is provided by the client
C. concentrate on what is being said
D. both listen to the client and accomplish other meaningful tasks at the same time

72) Which of the following is a latent function of the family unit?   72. _____

A. Economic production
B. Socialization of children
C. Provision of emotional support to members
D. Contribution to institutional arrangements

73) Current knowledge of post-traumatic stress disorder (PTSD) indicates that if the initial stage of anxiety and obsession with the trauma persist for longer than _____, the patient then enters stage 2, or acute PTSD.

A. 5–10 days
B. 4–6 weeks
C. 8–12 weeks
D. 3–6 months

74) After making contact with a person in crisis and establishing a relationship, a clinician faces the task of examining the dimensions of the problem, in order to define it. Which of the following is NOT typically a task of this phase of crisis intervention?   74. _____

A. Exploring alternatives
B. Assessing the dangerousness or lethality of the situation
C. Identifying the precipitating event that led to the crisis
D. Detailing a client's previous coping methods

75) In general, administrative evaluation at a social services agency differs from practice evaluation in that administrative evaluation is   75. _____

A. external to the supervisory relationship
B. continuous
C. basically self-contained
D. specific

KEY (CORRECT ANSWERS)

1.	B		41.	A
2.	C		42.	D
3.	C		43.	D
4.	C		44.	A
5.	D		45.	C
6.	D		46.	B
7.	A		47.	C
8.	B		48.	B
9.	D		49.	D
10.	B		50.	A
11.	C		51.	A
12.	C		52.	A
13.	C		53.	D
14.	D		54.	C
15.	A		55.	C
16.	B		56.	B
17.	D		57.	B
18.	C		58.	B
19.	C		59.	D
20.	A		60.	B
21.	D		61.	A
22.	C		62.	B
23.	D		63.	A
24.	D		64.	C
25.	A		65.	A
26.	B		66.	B
27.	B		67.	B
28.	B		68.	C
29.	B		69.	B
30.	B		70.	B
31.	A		71.	C
32.	A		72.	D
33.	A		73.	B
34.	D		74.	A
35.	D		75.	A
36.	D			
37.	A			
38.	B			
39.	A			
40.	D			

TEST 2

Directions: Each question or incomplete statement is followed by several suggested answers or completions. Select the one the BEST answers the question or completes the statement. *PRINT THE LETTER OF THE CORRECT ANSWER IN THE SPACE AT THE RIGHT.*

1) An 18-year-old girl is brought into a hospital emergency room by her family, who reported that she experienced sudden blindness. She had been arguing with her mother about why her mother was so much stricter with her than her father, when her mother suddenly blurted out that she and the father were seeking a divorce. The girl continued to argue for several minutes but then suddenly stopped and announced that she couldn't see anything. An examination reveals no neurological deficits. The client should most likely receive a diagnosis of

    1. _____

A.   conversion disorder
B.   somatoform disorder, not otherwise specified
C.   dissociative disorder
D.   hypochondriasis

2) An important difference between brief psychotherapy and crisis intervention is that

    2. _____

A.   brief therapy focuses on pathology
B.   crisis intervention focuses on specific issues
C.   brief therapy focuses on specific issues
D.   crisis intervention focuses on pathology

3) During an evaluation session in which the supervisor and practitioner are discussing the progress of the practitioner's current caseload, the practitioner admits to being unhappy with the overall progress of his clients, but attributes it to problems he has been experiencing because of excessive pressure placed on him by the supervisor. At this point in the evaluation, the supervisor should

    3. _____

A.   reassure the practitioner that whatever pressures have been placed on him have been for the benefit of his professional development
B.   apologize and suggest that the practitioner think of ways in which the supervisory relationship can be made more comfortable
C.   try to steer the focus of the discussion toward client progress
D.   remind the practitioner that he is the one ultimately responsible for handling the pressures that come with social work practice

4) In the time series design of program evaluation, the primary threat to internal validity is

    4. _____

A.   history
B.   selection
C.   testing
D.   regression to the mean

5) A client tells her clinician that members of an international espionage ring are after her to torture her and find out what she knows. She suspects that there are higher forces at work behind her persecution, but she can't tell the clinician what these forces are. Her beliefs have interfered with her work and social life for more than a year. The most appropriate diagnosis for this client is

5. _____

A. psychotic disorder, not otherwise specified
B. schizophrenia, paranoid type
C. delusional disorder
D. schizoaffective disorder

6) Which of the following factors is NOT typically associated with ethnicity?

6. _____

A. Language
B. Physical type
C. Economic status
D. Culture

7) A 19-year-old male client's father calls the social worker and requests information about his son's treatment. In this situation, the social worker should

7. _____

A. confirm that the son is in treatment but give no other information
B. tell the father about his son's progress but not reveal any specifics
C. set up a conjoint therapy session
D. refuse to reveal any information

8) In an approach-avoidance conflict, as the person nears the goal,

8. _____

A. attraction and aversion both increase
B. attraction and aversion both decrease
C. attraction increases and aversion decreases
D. atraction decreases and aversion increases

9) According the Herzberg's model of employee motivation, which of the following is a "hygiene" factor?

9. _____

A. Potential for growth
B. Interesting, challenging work
C. Freedom
D. Salary

10) A disturbance of consciousness accompanied by some changes in cognition is the distinguishing feature of

10. _____

A. schizophrenia
B. dementia
C. delusion
D. delirium

11)   Public and private social service agencies generally differ in each of   11. _____
the following ways, EXCEPT

A.   practitioner certification requirements
B.   philosophy of service
C.   service eligibility requirements
D.   scope of services

12)   Consistently, an employee is observed to be extremely friendly toward   12. _____
his boss, whom he really despises. From a Freudian perspective, the employee
is exhibiting

A.   reaction formation
B.   isolation of affect
C.   projection
D.   sublimation

13)   The purpose of an explanatory design for practice evaluation is to   13. _____

A.   determine the causes of specific client behaviors
B.   examine and reflect on the intervention being used
C.   examine the impact of the intervention on the target behavior
D.   monitor client progress

14)   Which of the following neurotransmitters or neuropeptides is generally   14. _____
deficient in clients with anorexia nervosa?

A.   Serotonin
B.   Cholecystokinin
C.   Dopamine
D.   Neuropeptide Y

15)   Services that are provided to clients without a means test are described as   15. _____

A.   pro-rated
B.   contributory
C.   eclectic
D.   universal

16)   In a family intervention formed in the strategic model, a clinician who   16. _____
uses a "restraining strategy" will begin the intervention by

A.   warning the family of the danger of continuing its symptomatic behavior
B.   directing the family to stop its symptomatic behavior
C.   warning the family of the negative consequences of behavioral change
D.   instructing the family to engage in only nonsymptomatic behavior

17)   The primary disadvantage associated with purchase-of-service agreements   17. _____
in social services is

A.   higher agency costs
B.   further fragmentation of the social service system
C.   decreased innovation in problem-solving
D.   diminished scope of services

18) Roles in the alcoholic family system have been labeled by Wegscheider   18. _____
and others. Typically, the youngest child in an alcoholic family occupies the role of

A.   mascot
B.   lost child
C.   hero
D.   scapegoat

19) The primary purpose for using confrontation in a client interview is to   19. _____

A.   teach mediation and conflict resolution skills
B.   activate the client's potential for change
C.   identify mixed messages in behaviors and thoughts or feelings
D.   identify the processes the client uses to make changes

20) A clinician at a mental health clinic decides to work from the perspective   20. _____
of Rogers client-centered therapy. If the counselor goes against the policy of the
clinic and decides to reject the use of diagnosis, it will be because from the person-
centered perspective,

A.   the validity of diagnostic labels has not been empirically demonstrated
B.   diagnosis forces the therapist, rather than the client, to assume the expert role
C.   labeling results in an incongruence between self and experience
D.   labeling discourages the process of in-depth interpretation of the client's behavior

21) Which of the following interventions is one of the most frequently used   21. _____
therapies in the treatment of phobias?

A.   Exposure therapy
B.   Object relations
C.   Extinction
D.   Social skills training

22) Which of the following statements about therapeutic group composition is   22. _____
generally FALSE?

A.   Task groups that are homogeneous are less productive and cohesive than
heterogeneous groups.
B.   Homogeneous groups of task-oriented, high-structure, impersonal people
function as effective, change-producing human relations groups.
C.   Heterogeneous encounter groups are more effective in producing greater self-
actualization of members.
D.   Homogeneous groups of person-oriented, low-structure people do not
generally function as effective human relations groups.

23) When behaviors are known and categorized prior to an observation, and   23. _____
the intention is to collect quantitative data, the method of choice is

A.   structured observation
B.   the Likert scale
C.   participant observation
D.   structured interview

24) A client who was abused as a child, whenever speaking of her parents,   24. _____
tends to cast the father in the most negative light possible, describing his as
evil and every encounter with him as a disaster. Of her mother, however, she
has only the most glowing praise, often referring to her as a saint. From a
psychodynamic perspective, the client is using the defense mechanism known as

A. reaction formation
B. primitive idealization
C. projection
D. splitting

25) In the transactional analysis model of social intercourse, the safest type   25. _____
of interaction is

A. a game
B. intimate
C. ritualistic
D. a pastime

26) Dissociative amnesia is usually   26. _____

    I. related to the inability to recall important personal information
    II. retrograde
    III. selective
    IV. accompanied by apraxia

A. I and II
B. II and III
C. I, II and III
D. II, III and IV

27) People often have difficulty receiving information because of an   27. _____
impairment or other barrier. Which of these will probably NOT help such a
person to better understand a message?

A. Repeating the message
B. Changing the sequence of the message
C. Changing the form in which the message is transmitted
D. Using an interpreter

28) A social worker is working with an autistic child who is mute. The   28. _____
major goal of intervention is the development of language. The social worker
begins by rewarding the child with food whenever he vocalizes. The social worker
then begins to reward the child only when his vocalizations occur within ten
seconds of the social worker's vocalization, then only if the child's vocalizations
resemble the social worker's, and so on, until the child's vocalizations are identical
to those of the social worker. The technique is used until the child is eventually
using words and sentences. This technique is known as:

A. counterconditioning
B. chaining
C. shaping
D. prompting

29) Potential limitations on confidentiality should be discussed with a client

29. _____

A. when the social worker determines it to be appropriate
B. at the onset of the professional relationship
C. at the onset of the professional relationship and thereafter as needed
D. and documented in writing as soon as possible

30) Other than describing a client's problem in a way that imposes meaning on a large amount of information, the primary cognitive task of assessment is to

30. _____

A. establish client comfort with the therapeutic plan
B. selectively focus on the information that will be most useful to the treatment planning process
C. infer whether a specific groups of facts or observations belongs to a larger known category of problems
D. identify the client's feelings of concern

31) The status of the practitioner/client therapeutic relationship is seen as an important aspect of therapy in each of the following models, EXCEPT

31. _____

A. ecosystems
B. psychoanalysis
C. client-centered
D. behavioral

32) Among the skills important to effective communication with clients, the most sophisticated and complex is/are

32. _____

A. encouraging, paraphrasing, and summarization
B. confrontation
C. influencing skills
D. open and closed questions

33) The _____ approach to human behavior attempts to describe behaviors in ways that allow for generalization across cultures.

33. _____

A. etic
B. holistic
C. emic
D. pluralist

34) The most widely-used bivariate statistical measure in social work is

34. _____

A. regression analysis
B. cross-tabulation
C. slope/drift
D. correlation

35) Which of the following statements is most abstract?

35. _____

A. Last night my mother told me I was a disappointment.
B. I cry all day long. I can't eat.
C. My daughter just sent me a letter.
D. My family is very close.

36) Each of the following is viewed by clinicians as an important element of the therapeutic relationship, EXCEPT

36. _____

A. confidentiality
B. dependability
C. sympathy
D. confidence

37) The _____ theory of human development holds that human behavior is strongly influenced by biology, is tied to evolution, and is characterized by critical and sensitive periods.

37. _____

A. Biosocial
B. Ecological
C. Social learning
D. Ethological

38) The residual model of social welfare

38. _____

I. is developed piecemeal as a reaction to the development of social problems, rather than in anticipation of them
II. views government as the last line of defense for people experiencing problems
III. views family and work as the first line of defense
IV. expects individuals to have trouble meeting the needs of modern living

A. I only
B. I and II
C. I, II, and III
D. I, II, III and IV

39) One of the helping models for multiproblem families is the Multiple-Impact Family-Therapy (MIFT) model, which includes each of the following elements, EXCEPT

39. _____

A. a long-term, client-centered approach
B. an extended session format
C. use of a team of professionals who work directly with the family
D. immediate response to a request for service

40) Which of the following has NOT been a factor in the recent growth of the for-profit sector of social services in the United States?

40. _____

A. The ability of for-profit agencies to offer more stable financial sources of income than other investments
B. The historical ability of private-sector solutions to solve problems that the government has failed to solve
C. The growing complexity and number of problems experienced by the disadvantaged
D. The existence of for-profit opportunities outside of public health insurance benefits

41)   Which of the following is NOT typically a factor used by private clinicians to determine fees for clients?

41. _____

A.   The amount charged by local psychiatrists of equal experience
B.   What the worker thinks will be the most attractive rate to the clientele she hopes to attract
C.   What third-party financing organizations identify as reasonable and customary charges
D.   How much other helping professionals charge for such services

42)   Erikson's final stage of psychosocial development, experienced during late adulthood, is

42. _____

A.   industry vs. inferiority
B.   generativity vs. stagnation
C.   intimacy vs. isolation
D.   integrity vs. despair

43)   Which of the following approaches to social services policymaking assess the process of moving from the identification of a social problem to implementing a policy and assessing the impact the policy has on the original problem?

43. _____

A.   Prescriptive
B.   Investment
C.   Cause and consequences
D.   Formative

44)   Research suggests that negative emotional effects from divorce are LEAST likely to impact

44. _____

A.   women who do not remarry
B.   women who remarry
C.   men who do not remarry
D.   men who remarry

45)   Closed questions typically do NOT begin with the word

45. _____

A.   how
B.   is
C.   do
D.   are

46)   In order to receive a diagnosis of acute stress disorder that conforms to DSM-IV standards, a client's symptoms must occur within _____ of a traumatic event.

46. _____

A.   5 days
B.   4 weeks
C.   3 months
D.   6 months

47)   Which of the following types of programs is typically administered   47. _____
exclusively at the county level?

A.   Food stamps
B.   AFDC
C.   Medical assistance
D.   General assistance

48)   In the clinical supervision of a social work practitioner, a good general   48. _____
policy is to

A.   begin with technical skill learning and then move to theoretical and
perspective learning
B.   begin with perspective learning and then move to technical skill learning
C.   teach a supervisee technical skills and theory simultaneously
D.   avoid both technical skills and theory and instead focus on smaller,
concrete problems faced by the practitioner

49)   Approximately what percentage of child maltreatment/abuse cases   49. _____
involve sexual abuse?

A.   5
B.   10
C.   30
D.   50

50)   In the United States, most social policy is formulated   50. _____

A.   by individual agency boards
B.   in a de facto manner by the direct practice of social workers
C.   through legislation
D.   by state boards

51)   Which of the following terms is used to describe memory loss that   51. _____
has a purely psychological cause?

A.   Anterograde
B.   Organic
C.   Retrograde
D.   Inorganic

52)   Which of the following statements reveals a client with a sensorimotor   52. _____
emotional orientation?

A.   A lot of us are angry. I know my boss is busy, but his forgetting to sign the payroll is
going to cost some of us our weekend plans.
B.   I'm feeling lost. I start to tremble when I go out in public.
C.   It seems that every time my wife is late meeting me somewhere, I get really angry with
her. My time is valuable.
D.   I feel really angry because my best friend borrowed my car without asking.

53) In order to receive a diagnosis of adjustment disorder that conforms to DSM-IV standards, a client's symptoms must occur within _____. of a traumatic event.

    53. _____

A. 5 days
B. 4 weeks
C. 3 months
D. 6 months

54) In the static-group comparison design of program evaluation, the primary threat to external validity is

    54. _____

A. maturation-treatment interaction
B. selection-treatment interaction
C. reactive effects
D. history-treatment interaction

55) According to Ainsworth, a "Type B" baby

    55. _____

A. exhibits insecurity by avoiding the mother
B. exhibits insecurity by resisting the mother
C. exhibits insecurity by clinging to the mother
D. uses the mother as a secure base from which to explore the environment

56) Which of the following is a primary social work setting?

    56. _____

A. Community center
B. Child protective services agency
C. Hospital
D. Nursing home

57) A client is a 40-year-old man who works as a night custodian at a local bank building. He keeps to himself and seems to have no interests outside his job, his stamp collection, and his two cats. He lives alone in a small apartment, has no close friends, and appears to have to interest in making friends. If this client is to receive a DSM-IV diagnosis, what would it be?

    57. _____

A. Avoidant personality disorder
B. Schizoid personality disorder
C. Antisocial personality disorder
D. No diagnosis--the man's isolation is not a disorder

58) A social or financial service that requires an applicant to prove financial need in order to receive the service is described as

    58. _____

A. means-tested
B. prescriptive
C. residual
D. eclectic

59)   The initial aim in treating a client with conversion disorder is   59. _____

A.   removal of the symptom
B.   determining predisposing factors
C.   forming a description of interpersonal relationships
D.   discovering precipitating stressors

60)   Which of the following is NOT a preexperimental design for   60. _____
program evaluation?

A.   One-group pretest/posttest
B.   Client satisfaction surveys
C.   Static-group comparison
D.   Solomon four-group approach

61)   In their definition of "family," many Asian Americans, especially   61. _____
Chinese Americans, are likely to include

I.   members of the nuclear family
II.   members of the extended family
III.   the informal network of community relations
IV.   all their ancestors and descendants

A.   I and II
B.   I, II and III
C.   I, II and IV
D.   I, II, III and IV

62)   Within the context of the therapeutic relationship, practitioners and clients   62. _____
deal either explicitly or implicitly with

I.   past experiences that have affected abilities to relate to others
II.   the present physical, emotional, and perceptual state of the transaction
III.   each person's expectations of the process

A.   I only
B.   I and II
C.   II and III
D.   I, II and II

63)   Assertiveness and social skills training are interventions MOST likely   63. _____
to be useful to clients with

A.   panic disorder with agoraphobia
B.   avoidant personality disorder
C.   narcissistic personality disorder
D.   schizoid personality disorder

64) A client reports to a practitioner at an outpatient care clinic in clear psychological distress, exhibiting paranoia and severe anxiety. The clinician is certain that the client has some form of anxiety disorder. The patient has severe liver disease, but the clinician can't determine whether this is a factor; it's possible that the problem is related to other factors such as the client's persistent substance abuse. The most likely DSM-IV diagnosis would be Anxiety Disorder,

64. _____

A. provisional
B. not otherwise specified
C. with generalized anxiety
D. undifferentiated

65) Which of the following is NOT generally a guideline for supervisors to follow regarding case presentation?

65. _____

A. The presentation should be organized around questions to be answered.
B. The supervisor should present a case first.
C. The presentation should progress from practitioner dynamics to client dynamics.
D. The presentation should be based on written or audiovisual material.

66) A thirty-five-year-old client was referred by a friend because of her sadness and talk of suicide, which were brought on by the death of her lover several years ago but never fully subsided. A practitioner working from the existential viewpoint would view the goal of assessment with this client as

66. _____

A. an in-depth understanding of her subjective experience
B. identifying the support resources already available to her
C. the identification of situations and stimuli that reinforce her depressive responses
D. achieving transference

67) Which of the following processes typically occurs LATEST in the therapeutic relationship?

67. _____

A. Individuation
B. Idealization
C. Individualization
D. Identification

68) A social worker has been seeing a client who whose wife left him and moved out of state with the children. During a session, the client says he wishes he could find out where she lives, so he could make her pay for what she's done. The social worker should

68. _____

A. call domestic violence experts and document the statement
B. call domestic violence experts and get legal advice
C. call the police
D. try to find the ex-wife and warn her

69)   Some Marxist-oriented behavioral theorists believe that when individuals   69. _____
meet in face-to-face encounters, they make several different adaptations. For
example, when individuals of different classes meet, the interaction tends to be
very narrow and role-prescribed. This is an example of _____
generalization.

A.   means-end
B.   feelings
C.   control-purposiveness
D.   detachment

70)   A practitioner using rational-emotive therapy to help a child who is   70. _____
depressed has gathered information from the child's parents and teachers,
and has collected formal assessment instruments that were completed by the
parents and the child. The practitioner then meets with the parents and the child
together, and asks the parents a series of questions about their child's symptoms
and their history of attempts to deal with the problem. The practitioner's NEXT
step should be to

A.   question both the parents and the child about treatment goals
B.   assess the parents and the child for secondary disturbance
C.   ask for the child's opinion of her parents' statements
D.   assess the practical and/or emotional problems presented

71)   The record-keeping requirements at a typical social services   71. _____
agency require the completion of progress notes at an interval no longer than

A.   after every client contact
B.   weekly
C.   every 30 days
D.   every 90 days

72)   NASW policy regarding foster care and transracial adoption states   72. _____
that placement decisions should reflect a child's need for

A.   basic material comforts
B.   continuity
C.   ethnic/racial integrity
D.   a stimulating, challenging environment

73)   Which of the following statements about the behavioral approach   73. _____
to treatment is FALSE?

A.   Behavioral interventions are intended to modify only certain, limited
aspects of human behavior
B.   Under certain conditions, behaviorists are concerned with affect and
cognitions
C.   Behaviorists prefer observation over introspection
D.   Behaviorists believe that a client's symptoms are merely observable
behaviors that have been labeled as problematic

74)   Within the family life-cycle perspective, divorces are sometimes   74. _____
referred to as

A.   derailments
B.   dislocations
C.   non-normative crises
D.   ruptures

75)   Which of the following statements is TRUE regarding summative   75. _____
program evaluations?

A.   Interpretive approaches using qualitative data are particularly useful.
B.   They make no attempt to determine causality.
C.   Validity is a central concern.
D.   Evaluations provide detail about a program's strengths and weaknesses.

_____

KEY (CORRECT ANSWERS)

1. A		41. A
2. A		42. D
3. C		43. C
4. A		44. A
5. B		45. A
6. C		46. B
7. D		47. D
8. A		48. A
9. D		49. B
10. D		50. C
11. A		51. A
12. A		52. B
13. C		53. C
14. C		54. B
15. D		55. D
16. C		56. B
17. B		57. B
18. A		58. A
19. B		59. A
20. B		60. D
21. A		61. C
22. A		62. D
23. A		63. B
24. D		64. B
25. C		65. C
26. C		66. A
27. B		67. A
28. C		68. B
29. C		69. A
30. C		70. C
31. D		71. C
32. C		72. B
33. A		73. A
34. B		74. B
35. D		75. C
36. C		
37. D		
38. C		
39. A		
40. C		

EXAMINATION SECTION

Directions: Each question or incomplete statement is followed by several suggested answers or completions. Select the one that BEST answers the question or completes the statement. *PRINT THE LETTER OF THE CORRECT ANSWER IN THE SPACE AT THE RIGHT.*

1) During an assessment interview, a practitioner attempts to determine a client's "executive functioning." This means mostly the degree to which a client is able to

    I.   live without stress
    II.   act in a leadership role
    III.   organize and implement activities
    IV.   deal with multiple responsibilities

A.   I and IV
B.   II only
C.   III and IV
D.   I, II, III and IV

1. _____

2) Most likely, family therapy would be the primary intervention of choice for each of the following, EXCEPT

A.   borderline personality issues
B.   individual problems related to family transitions
C.   problems in relationships
D.   problems with children

2. _____

3) About _____ of today's elderly population suffer from mental health problems.

A.   1/8
B.   1/4
C.   1/2
D.   3/4

3. _____

4) In interpersonal communication, responses such as ignoring a client, cutting him off in mid-sentence, changing the subject, reacting ambiguously, or being condescending can cause the client to value himself less. These types of responses are described as

A.   low-context
B.   toxic
C.   polarizing
D.   disconfirming

4. _____

5)   Nearly all forms of therapeutic relationships involve   5. _____

     I.   a suspension of moral judgment
     II.   constancy of the clinician's interest no matter how disturbing
          the subject
     III.   the practitioner allowing him/herself to be used as a transfer-
          ence object without the interference of counter-transference
     IV.   the client's opportunity to speak the unspeakable

A.   I and II
B.   II and IV
C.   III and IV
D.   I, II, III and IV

6)   Personality assessments are most often categorized as either   6. _____

A.   verbal and performance
B.   behavioral and psychodynamic
C.   projective or objective
D.   social or vocational

7)   _____ theory holds that it is a person's own   7. _____
unrealistic beliefs that generate a fear of failure.

A.   Systematic desensitization
B.   Empowerment
C.   Performance visualization
D.   Cognitive restructuring

8)   What is the psychoanalytic term for the release of emotional energy   8. _____
related to unconscious conflicts?

A.   Dam-breaking
B.   Projection
C.   Catharsis
D.   Transference

9)   According to the model of Rational-Emotive Behavior Therapy   9. _____
(REBT), which of the following would be an example of a core irrational
belief?

A.   One should keep the focus on the present
B.   One must have perfect and definite self-control.
C.   No matter how bad it is, it will be over shortly.
D.   Things could always be worse.

10) Regarding professional consultation with colleagues about clients, the NASW code of ethics establishes the rule of thumb that social workers should

10. _____

A. avoid consultation in cases where the client is known to be violent
B. disclose the least amount of information to achieve the purposes of the consultation
C. disclose no confidential or potentially sensitive information to consultants
D. make sure consulting professionals know as much as they do about the client before offering input into the case

11) To help female clients understand the ecosystems that affect their well-being, social work practitioners should use

11. _____

A. gender role analysis, to help women understand their relations with men
B. stereotypes, to consider male-female interactions
C. an androcentric knowledge base, to assess the experiences of women
D. female biology and endocrinology, to explain emotional and behavioral responses

12) The use of psychological tests in clinical social work should be governed by the idea that

12. _____

I. clients should be involved in the test-selection process whenever possible or feasible
II. a client should be made aware that tests are only tools, and will not provide any answers to the client's problems in and of themselves
III. test results, and not merely scores, should always be released and explained to the client
IV. clients' reasons for wanting tests, as well as their past experiences with tests, should be explored before selecting any assessment

A. I and II
B. II only
C. II and IV
D. I, II, III and IV

13) In Adlerian therapy, client nonverbal behaviors are often used to assess

13. _____

A. ego states
B. self-talk
C. hidden purposes of behaviors
D. conflicts or discrepancies

14)   In the behavioral model, maladjustment results from   14. _____

A.   personality defects
B.   flawed learning
C.   heredity
D.   environmental barriers

15)   Despite broad-based application and compatibility with social work   15. _____
values, evidence-based practice approaches are not universally accepted in
clinical settings. Each of the following is a significant reason for this, EX-
CEPT

A.   clinician reluctance
B.   clinician unfamiliarity with empirical data collection methods
C.   lack of organizational availability
D.   client concerns

16)   Which of the following is a structured personality assessment?   16. _____

A.   Thematic Apperception Test (TAT)
B.   Minnesota Multiphasic Personality Inventory (MMPI)
C.   Sentence Completion Test
D.   Rorschach

17)   An client must provide informed consent for psychological treatment   17. _____
if

        I.   treatment may have positive or negative effects
        II.   one treatment is not superior to another
        III.   treatment may be hazardous
        IV.   full cooperation is required for success of therapy

A.   I and II
B.   II only
C.   II, III and IV
D.   I, II, III and IV

18)   According to Sullivan, dysfunctional families seek   18. _____

A.   security rather than satisfaction
B.   gratification rather than democracy
C.   power rather than cohesion
D.   avoidance rather than engagement

19) During a client interview, a practitioner wants to transition from his own preliminary comments and prompt a response from the client. Which of the following is NOT generally recognized as a gesture that would signify "turn yielding?"

19. _____

A. Talking more loudly
B. Asking a direct question
C. Slowing the rate of speech
D. Terminating body movements and gazing at the client

20) Among Asian Americans, mental illness is often expressed as

20. _____

A. adjustment disorder
B. borderline personality disorder
C. psychosomatic complaint
D. depression

21) In the *Diagnostic and Statistical Manual of Mental Disorders* (DSM-IV), diagnoses are a process of elimination. This means that a clinician

21. _____

I. arrives at diagnoses by eliminating differential diagnoses
II. must adopt an attitude of skepticism when making a tentative diagnosis
III. starts with many possible diagnostic categories, and through multiple observations eliminates each of them until only one remains
IV. arrives at a diagnosis by determining how many symptoms the person has in common with what's published for a particular DSM diagnosis

A. I and II
B. I and III
C. II and IV
D. IV only

22. _____

22) The psychoanalytic perspective holds that the infant's emergent sense of self begins in the

A. uterus
B. first two months of life
C. first year of life
D. first two years of life

23)   After a client's presenting problem has been diagnosed, a social
worker begins planning for service delivery. The FIRST step in this process is
typically to

A.   identify services
B.   develop a plan for services
C.   conduct additional interviews and tests
D.   revisit the assessment/diagnosis phase

23. _____

24)   When a clinician asks his client to lie down on a couch and talk about
whatever comes to mind, he is using the technique of

A.   transference
B.   catharsis
C.   free association
D.   response shaping

24. _____

25)   Which of the following is NOT usually part of a process recording?

A.   Recorder's feelings and reactions
B.   Observations
C.   Quotations, to the extent that they can be remembered
D.   Diagnosis

25. _____

26)   A mildly retarded male client lives in a resident facility and is sexually
active. He has impregnated two young women at the facility, and one of the
resident clinicians is recommending that the client's family consider persuad-
ing him to get a vasectomy. This case will most likely involve the ethical and
legal issue of

A.   duty to warn
B.   informed consent
C.   due process
D.   confidentiality

26. _B_

27)   Which of the following is NOT developed during infancy?

A.   Telegraphic speech
B.   Transductive reasoning
C.   Separation anxiety
D.   Object permanence

27. _____

28) A client tells a practitioner: "One of the reasons I quit my job was because my boss was always pushing me. I could never say no to her. Whatever she wanted, I always gave in. I think it's hard to say no to people until I reach a point where I can't take it any more."

The practitioner responds with the following summary of the client's statement: "You're discovering that you tend to give in or not do what you'd like until you become angry and break things off—not just in your working relationships, but in other relationships as well." This is an example of a summary whose purpose is to

A. tie together multiple elements of a message
B. review progress
C. identify a theme
D. regulate the pace of the session

28. _____

29) Each of the following is a common form of countertransference that can occur in the treatment of clients, EXCEPT the

A. focus on feeling liked and appreciated by the client
B. reluctance to give advice because of a fear of creating a sense of dependence
C. strong reaction to certain clients who evoke negative emotions in the practitioner
D. reluctance to challenge a client because it might result in resentment or other negative feelings

29. _____

30) In Baumrind's model of parenting styles, the happiest and best-behaved children usually have parents who use the _____ style of parenting.

A. permissive
B. authoritarian
C. disciplinarian
D. authoritative

30. _____

31) During an assessment interview, a practitioner asks a client: "In what kind of situations do you find it easier to manage or control this reaction?" The practitioner is attempting to identify

A. secondary gains associated with the presenting problem
B. client resources and strengths
C. consequences of the problem
D. antecedents to the problem

31. _____

32) Interpersonal psychotherapy has proven effective in the treatment of   32. _B_

A. schizophrenia
B. depression
C. phobias
D. bipolar disorder

33) In the social service system, collaboration   33. _____

    I. may involve community planning
    II. is achieved both formally and informally
    III. is most prominently illustrated among the work of clinic teams
    IV. increases treatment effectiveness by combining competencies

A. I and III
B. I, II and IV
C. II and IV
D. I, II, III and IV

34) Dysthymia is considered to be associated with a greater risk of suicide   34. _____
when it occurs in

A. women
B. children
C. older men
D. in conjunction with a personality disorder

35) A clinician suspects that a ten-year-old boy may be suffering from   35. _D_
neglect. For children of this age, common indicators of neglect include

    I. refusal to even attempt homework assignments
    II. crying easily when hurt even slightly
    III. falling asleep in class
    IV. consistently showing up early to school

A. I and II
B. I, II and III
C. III only
D. I, II, III and IV

36) Minor clients—those under the age of consent—are considered to have   36. _____

A. a legal right to privacy
B. an ethical right to privacy
C. both an ethical and legal right to privacy
D. deferred their right to privacy to their parents, who deserve to know
the details of the intervention process

37) The use of probes is often helpful for either expanding or narrowing the parameters of discussions with clients. The FIRST step in formulating an effective probe is often to

37. _____

A. determine the purpose of the probe
B. decide what type of question will be most helpful
C. use a paraphrase or reflection response
D. determine what the client needs to know or do

38) In Watson and Tellegen's map of the human emotions, the emotions that are most closely related are

38. _____

A. pleasure and pain
B. surprise and relaxation
C. disappointment and relief
D. anger and fear

39) Helping a client to recognize and mobilize her own coping resources and available supportive network of friends and family is an example of the _____ effect of social support

39. C

A. buffering
B. transactional
C. direct
D. indirect

40) A working alliance with a client is said to be necessarily composed of each of the following, EXCEPT

40. _____

A. an emotional bond between client and practitioner
B. agreement on therapeutic goals
C. agreement on the practitioner's leadership role in planning and conducting interventions
D. agreement on therapeutic tasks

41) Cognitive therapy has proven to be effective in the treatment of

41. _____

I. major depression
II. eating disorders
III. anxiety disorders
IV. panic disorders

A. I and II
B. II only
C. II and III
D. I, II, III and IV

42)   De-institutionalization, as it applies to mental health practices, involves the concept of the "least restrictive alternative." This concepts basically means that

42. _____

A.   professionals should only commit clients who are delusional
B.   at least one less restrictive alternative must be attempted before voluntary commitment is sought
C.   practitioners should select a mode of treatment that gives them the
greatest possible latitude in making decisions about a client's future
D.   treatment should be no more intrusive or harsher than necessary in
order to achieve therapeutic aims and protect clients and others from physical
harm

43)   Post-traumatic stress disorder falls under the category of _____
___ disorders.

43. _____

A.   dissociative
B.   mood
C.   somatoform
D.   anxiety

44)   The stereotypes that lock Americans into traditional gender activities
are MOST likely to be broken by

44. _____

A.   equal pay for equal work
B.   greater male participation in family-oriented, nurturing activities
C.   greater female participation in institutional decision-making
D.   more stringent anti-discrimination legislation

45)   _____ theories of ethics claim that certain actions are
simply right or wrong as a matter of fundamental principle.

45. _____

A.   Teleological
B.   Consequentialist
C.   Deontological
D.   Utilitarian

46)   Which of the following is an Axis II disorder?

46. _____

A.   Major Depression
B.   Separation Anxiety Disorder
C.   Mental retardation
D.   Panic Disorder

47) One of the most common dysfunctions of the nuclear family is that it can create   47. _____

A. a generation gap
B. institutional fragmentation
C. a breakdown of authority
D. emotional overload

48) The frequency with which a clinical social work practitioner receives supervision should depend on each of the following, EXCEPT the   48. _____

A. level of the practitioner's training and experience
B. worker's activities
C. expectations of the supervisor
D. agreement in theoretical perspective between supervisor and practitioner

49) _____ personality theories are based on the premise that predispositions direct the behavior of a person in a consistent pattern.   49. _____

A. Psychodynamic
B. Behavioral
C. Trait
D. Humanistic

50) When a communicative response is given that matches a client's previous communication, the _____ is established.   50. _____

A. halo effect
B. valence
C. norm of reciprocity
D. boundary elimination

51) Which of the following standardized assessment tools is a Likert-type self-report measure that assesses overall health or pathology in a general score?   51. _____

A. *McMaster Family Assessment Device*
B. *Parenting Stress Index*
C. *Family Environment Scale*
D. *Dyadic Cohesion Scale*

52)   Which of the following theories are most relevant to the humanistic-experiential model of treatment?   52. _____

A.   Rational-emotive behavior therapy (REBT) and choice theory
B.   Gestalt therapy and person-centered treatment
C.   Freudian and Jungian theory
D.   Cognitive theory and behavioral theory

53)   The principle that two people in a continuing relationship—such as a social worker and a client—feel a strong obligation to repay their social debts to one another is the   53. _____

A.   Hawthorne effect
B.   law of empathy
C.   norm of reciprocity
D.   law of effect

54)   In a therapeutic encounter, which of the following client behaviors is most likely to be interpreted as a "retroflection" by a Gestalt therapist?   54. _____

A.   Not making eye contact
B.   Laughing off important things
C.   Speaking abstractly or indirectly
D.   Holding the breath

55)   Verbal means of conveying empathy to a client include   55. _____

        I.   using verbal responses that refer to the client's feelings
        II.   using verbal responses that bridge or add on to implicit client messages
        III.   placing the client's presenting problems in a clinical context
        IV.   explaining the client's emotions

A.   I and II
B.   I, II and III
C.   II and III
D.   I, II, III and IV

56)   Conflict theorists assert that unity that is present in society is the result of   56. _____

A.   consensus
B.   competition
C.   contract
D.   coercion

57)   Confrontation can be a useful tool with clients who are unable or   57. _____
unwilling to face up to the realities of their own thoughts or feelings, but it is
also a response that requires great vigilance and judiciousness on the part of
the clinician. In describing a distortion or a discrepancy to a client, a clinician
should NOT

A.   use a confrontation to vent frustration with a client's behaviors
B.   cite a specific example of the behavior, rather than a generalized infer-
ence
C.   avoid confronting near the end of a therapy session
D.   attempt to determine the client's willingness to change before present-
ing a challenge

58)   In family systems theory, "first-order" change occurs only when   58. _____

A.   the family's own narrative about their behavior changes
B.   the rules of the system change
C.   a feedback loop becomes evident
D.   a specific behavior in within the system changes

59)   One principle of human behavior is that when people are observed, or   59. _____
believe someone is paying close attention, they behave differently. This phenomenon is known as

A.   role ambiguity
B.   the Peter principle
C.   self-perception bias
D.   the Hawthorne effect

60)   During the service delivery process, a referral can sometimes fail to   60. _____
result in a positive client outcome. Which of the following is LEAST likely to
be a reason for this failure?

A.   Insufficient practitioner knowledge of resources
B.   Countertransference from referring practitioner
C.   Practitioner misjudgement of client's capability to follow through with
referral
D.   Practitioner insensitivity to, or misjudgement of, client needs

61)   For children, the factor with the highest predictive value for social   61. _____
problems is

A.   ethnicity
B.   poverty
C.   education
D.   substance abuse

62) A practitioner has administered two separate standardized psychological assessments to a client. When considering the release of this assessment
data to third parties, the practitioner

62. _____

A. release the data only to those competent to interpret them
B. may release the data to anyone who asks for it
C. should keep in mind that other practitioners can release assessment
data transferred to them by the practitioner
D. are not obligated to monitor the release of assessment data

63) Each of the following is a typical function served by the family unit,
EXCEPT to

63. _____

A. provide for children's basic needs
B. indoctrinate children in the ways of society
C. act as the primary agent of socialization
D. provide a uniform plan for socializing children

64) Social work supervisors who are attempting to evaluate their own
questioning techniques with supervisees should be sure they

64. _____

A. ensure thorough case knowledge before moving on to questions related
to intervention strategies
B. preface individual questions with introductory statements
C. ask questions in a general way in order to receive general answers
D. make sure that questions related to intervention strategies and tech-
niques are more specific that questions about diagnostic understanding

65) In its formulations, the *Diagnostic and Statistical Manual of Mental
Disorders* (DSM-IV) relies on

65. _____

    I. a medical model of human development
    II. an empirical array of the opinions of many diagnosticians
    III. a strengths model of human development
    IV. the opinions of a designated board of diagnosticians who share
         similar theoretical perspectives

A. I and II
B. II only
C. II and III
D. IV only

66) A clinician and a client are in the middle phase of a task-centered intervention. At the beginning of each session, they will   66. _D_

A.   establish incentives and rationales for tasks
B.   identify obstacles to task accomplishment
C.   engage in guided practice and rehearsal
D.   review problems and tasks to determine progress

67) An adolescent boy, shortly after his release from a reformatory for juvenile delinquents, commits an act of vandalism. The boy feels it is in his nature to commit such acts, because he has been identified as a "juvenile delinquent" by society. His act of vandalism is an example of   67. _B_

A.   primary deviance
B.   secondary deviance
C.   stigmatization
D.   a cry for help

68) What is the immediate short-term effect of a tricyclic antidepressant?   68. _A_

A.   Increasing the availability of serotonin and norepinephrine in synapses
B.   Dampening the CNS arousal state
C.   Reducing intracranial pressure by reducing cerebrospinal fluid
D.   Increasing available lithium in the bloodstream for absorption

69) A practitioner needs to wrap up a 50-minute session with a client in order to prepare for her next session. Of the following, the BEST closing to a session is   69. _B_

A.   I'm sorry this divorce has been so difficult for you. Let's pick up with that feeling next week.
B.   I see we have about ten minutes left together. Let's try to come up with some strategies that you can work on for next week.
C.   I see we have about ten minutes remaining in this session. Let's see if we can't address your drug problem to some extent before we say goodbye.
D.   It's 2:50 and my next client is in the office. Let's see if we can wrap this up together.

70) Which of the following theoretical perspectives provides a kind of bridge between psychoanalysis and family therapy?   70. _A_

A.   Object relations
B.   Ego identity
C.   Self psychology
D.   Family dynamism

71)   When giving feedback to a client, it is usually NOT advisable to   71. _____

A.   claim clear ownership of the comment
B.   be specific
C.   focus on personality traits
D.   note a behavior

72)   Society typically neutralizes deviant behaviors in each of the following   72. _____
ways, EXCEPT by

A.   denying responsibilities
B.   denying victimhood
C.   appealing to higher loyalties
D.   denying deviant labels

73)   A client, referred to a clinician, is covered by her insurer for a total   73. _____
of eight treatment sessions. The client is an incest victim, and the clinician
believes it will take more sessions than this to help her with her problems. He
decides to offer the client his services pro bono. The practitioner's decision is
an illustration of the principle of

A.   self-determination
B.   fidelity
C.   justice
D.   due process

74)   Each of the following is true of psychiatric inpatient care, EXCEPT   74. _____
that it

A.   can be combined with social systems intervention
B.   is increasingly associated with legal mandates
C.   is usually appropriate only for medical problems
D.   can often be shortened by crisis intervention

75)   During an interview, a client says: "My life is really boring. There's nothing new going on and all my friends are away. I wish I had enough money to make something happen."

The clinician has decided that the Adlerian approach will be most useful with this client. Which of the following interpretations of the above statement is most in line with the Adlerian approach?

A.   "You seem to be saying you don't know how to enjoy yourself without having other people around. Maybe recognizing this will help you learn to be more self-reliant."

B.   "Sounds as if you need excitement, friends, and money to make your life seem worthwhile."

C.   "It seems as if you can only be happy when you're able to play and have fun. The child in you seems to be in control of a good part of your life."

D.   "You seem to think things are terrible because you have no friends around now, and no money. Is there any proof for that? I think your feelings of boredom might change if you could draw a different and more logical conclusion from your circumstances."

75. _____

KEY (CORRECT ANSWERS)

1.	C	41.	D
2.	A	42.	D
3.	B	43.	D
4.	D	44.	C
5.	D	45.	C
6.	C	46.	C
7.	D	47.	D
8.	C	48.	D
9.	B	49.	C
10.	B	50.	C
11.	A	51.	A
12.	D	52.	B
13.	C	53.	C
14.	B	54.	D
15.	B	55.	A
16.	B	56.	D
17.	D	57.	A
18.	A	58.	D
19.	A	59.	D
20.	C	60.	B
21.	B	61.	B
22.	B	62.	A
23.	D	63.	D
24.	C	64.	A
25.	D	65.	A
26.	B	66.	D
27.	B	67.	B
28.	C	68.	A
29.	B	69.	B
30.	D	70.	A
31.	B	71.	C
32.	B	72.	D
33.	D	73.	C
34.	B	74.	C
35.	D	75.	B
36.	B		
37.	C		
38.	D		
39.	A		
40.	C		

TEST 2

Directions: Each question or incomplete statement is followed by several suggested answers or completions. Select the one that BEST answers the question or completes the statement. *PRINT THE LETTER OF THE CORRECT ANSWER IN THE SPACE AT THE RIGHT.*

1)   In which of the following cases is treatment considered to be "mandated?"

    1. _____

    I.   The court orders a person to attend treatment sessions, with consequences for noncompliance
    II.   Concerned neighbors insist that a child who is disruptive in the community be evaluated for a mental illness or disturbance
    III.   Parents withhold college tuition if their child does not check into a drug rehabilitation facility
    IV.   A spouse threatens to leave if a partner does not seek treatment

A.   I only
B.   I and II
C.   I, II, and III
D.   I, II, III and IV

2)   Two types of psychological tests that are the most commonly used in clinical practice are

    2. _____

A.   cognitive/ability and personality
B.   interest surveys and vocational skills
C.   conscious and unconscious
D.   speech perception and reaction time

3)   The emphasis of contemporary psychodynamic approaches to treatment tends to be

    3. _____

A.   interpersonal functioning
B.   repressed sexuality
C.   long-term treatment
D.   childhood events

4)   A significant concept in the contemporary psychoanalytic view of families is the idea of a family as a

    4. _____

A.   sociological dimension
B.   group of interconnected intrapsychic systems
C.   cacophony of competing ids
D.   single organic entity focused on self-preservation

5)   Assumptions associated with the practice of professional consultation   5. _____
include each of the following, EXCEPT

A.   Consultation may result in confirming the rightness of the clinician's
current actions.
B.   The consultant has greater knowledge than the consultee in the areas
of agency and worker needs.
C.   In order to work positively, consultation cannot be compelled
D.   Consultation is made more effective when the consultant provides
feedback to the employer or agency about the consultee's skills.

6)   Together, practitioner and client have identified the client's needs and   6. _____
corresponding services. The practitioner then turns his attention to resource
selection. Typically, the paramount decision-making concern in resource
selection is the

A.   capacity of the practitioner to treat the presenting problem(s)
B.   information and referral system
C.   agency's policies and procedures
D.   client's values and preferences

7)   Of the following concepts, the one that most clearly is derived from   7. _____
the theoretical intersection between dynamic psychiatry and the social sci-
ences is that

        I.   culture influences personality
        II.   role performance is an effect of personality
        III.   social class will affect a person's response to stress

A.   I only
B.   I and II
C.   II and III
D.   I, II and III

8)   The most prominent model for budgeting within human services orga-   8. _____
nizations includes each of the following categories, EXCEPT

A.   subcontracts
B.   distribution and control
C.   recording and reporting
D.   acquisitions

9)   A schizophrenic client who _____ would be con-   9. _____
sidered to be at an increased risk for suicide.

A.   is female
B.   recently discharged from a hospital
C.   is older
D.   has manic symptoms

10)   The distinctive quality of antipsychotic drugs is their ability to   10. _____

A.   calm clients down
B.   elevate dopamine levels
C.   reduce the intensity of delusions and hallucinations
D.   reduce feelings of anxiety

11)   In the *Diagnostic and Statistical Manual of Mental Disorders* (DSM-   11. _____
IV), a diagnosis of alcohol dependency

        I.   is less severe than a diagnosis of alcohol abuse
        II.   requires that the person does not have control over use
        III.   requires only that the person regularly drinks to excess
        IV.   requires a disruption of socio-economic functionings

A.   I and II
B.   II and IV
C.   III only
D.   III and IV

12)   The FACES II is a standardized assessment tool in which members   12. _____
rate their families on the dimensions of

A.   conflict and cohesion
B.   cohesion and adaptability
C.   crisis-orientation and resilience
D.   adaptability and dysfunction

13)   Records of client and practitioner behavior that are clinically rele-   13. _____
vant—including interventions used, client responses to treatments, the evolution of the treatment plan, and any follow-up measures taken—are usually
referred to as

A.   screening data
B.   progress notes
C.   baseline data
D.   assessments

14) During a session with his clinician, a 68-year-old client, who has confessed to becoming more withdrawn in recent years, describes his life as a "list of vaguely worded goals, all unachieved." Which of Erikson's stages does the client illustrate?

14. _____

A. basic trust vs. mistrust
B. intimacy vs. isolation
C. integrity vs. despair
D. generativity vs. stagnation

15) The definition of psychotherapy includes each of the following characteristics, EXCEPT that it

15. _____

A. is conducted by a trained professional
B. relies on medical treatment methods
C. is based on psychological theory
D. uses psychological methods

16) _____ explanation of aggression involves the process of catharsis.

16. _____

A. The social learning
B. The frustration-aggression
C. Freud's
D. Jung's

17) A diagnosis of dementia requires that a clinician examine a client for

17. _____

A. aphasia
B. alogia
C. ataxia
D. encephalitis

18) For Americans older than 65, isolation becomes a problem, especially for

18. _____

A. women
B. ethnic minorities
C. immigrants
D. the disabled

19)   A practitioner is beginning to suspect that the multiple injuries she has   19. _____
observed over a twelve-week period with an eight-year-old client may be the
result of abuse. Because the child's family is from another culture with which
the practitioner is admittedly unfamiliar, she decides not to report her suspi-
cions to the authorities, and instead decides to address the abuse as part of her
family treatment plan. The practitioner has

A.   broken the law
B.   demonstrated cultural competency
C.   shown the proper respect for the family's right to self-determination
D.   unethically shifted the focus of her intervention

20)   Which of the following is a contemporary neo-Freudian form of psy-   20. _____
chotherapy that ignores unconscious motivation?

A.   Interpersonal psychotherapy
B.   Systematic desensitization
C.   Assertiveness training
D.   Social skills training

21)   Human services organizations tend to have a unique set of characteris-   21. _____
tics that represent significant challenges to manager, including

    I.   a mixture of private benefits for services users and public ben-
           efits for society
    II.   dependence on external constituencies over which members
           have little control
    III.   a determinate set of technologies, with predictable outcomes
    IV.   core activities that involve interactive transactions between
           staff members and users of services

A.   I only
B.   I, II and IV
C.   III and IV
D.   I, II, III and IV

22)   Which of the following refers to the elements of a person's position in   22. _____
society that have exceptional significance to her social identity?

A.   Role
B.   Niche markers
C.   Posting
D.   Master status

23) During a client interview, a practitioner notices a consistent discrepancy between what a client is saying and her nonverbal behaviors. Pointing out this discrepancy is an example of a response known as

23. _____

A. reflecting feeling
B. interpretation
C. clarification
D. confrontation

24) Systematic desensitization and graded exposure are two techniques that are used to treat

24. _____

A. bipolar disorder
B. depression
C. phobias
D. schizophrenia

25) The perspective that attributes a person's place in the society as a function of innate ability is

25. _____

A. labeling theory
B. cultural transmission
C. social Darwinism
D. conflict theory

26) The Gestalt model of therapy views awareness as

26. _____

A. healing
B. impossible
C. a schema
D. an inherently inhibitory process

27) The goal of a projective assessment is to

27. _____

A. evaluate the way a person perceives ambiguous stimuli
B. predict a person's behavior
C. compare a person's responses to those of other persons with similar presenting problems or disorders
D. evaluate the degree to which organic factors influence a person's thinking

28) In structural family therapy, the tool used by the clinician to observe and modify problematic family patterns is the

28. _____

A. family narrative
B. ecomap
C. differential diagnosis
D. enactment

29) Without the expression of warmth in the clinician/client relationship, particular strategies and helping interventions are likely to be

29. _____

A. more in line with the client's expectations that with the practitioner's
B. helpful only to clients from low-context cultures
C. technically correct but therapeutically useless
D. perceived as abstract challenges by the client

30) As described by Robert Merton, typically human responses to anomie include each of the following, EXCEPT

30. _____

A. rebellion
B. conformity
C. ritualism
D. recidivism

31) A clinician in object relations practice encounters a client who was abused as a child. The client believes the only way she can improve her situation is to change herself. The client is likely to solve this object-related dilemma by

31. _____

A. openly contemplating the abuse and its implications
B. unconsciously repressing the abuse
C. dividing the object into good and bad parts and then internalizing the bad aspects
D. lying to the clinician about the abuse

32) Clinical scales of the Minnesota Multiphasic Personality Inventory (MMPI) include each of the following, EXCEPT the _____ _ scale.

32. _____

A. marital distress
B. depression
C. paranoia
D. hypochondriasis

33) For legal purposes, a practitioner's "records" include   33. _____

    I.   audiotapes of sessions
    II.   case notes
    III.   appointment books
    IV.   intake forms

A.   I and II
B.   II and IV
C.   II, III and IV
D.   I, II, III and IV

34) According to the transactional analysis model, each of the following   34. _____
describes the adult ego state, in transactional analysis, EXCEPT

A.   calculating
B.   instructive
C.   unemotional
D.   rational

35) Evidence suggests that the largest source of human service delivery in   35. _____
the area of mental health is the

A.   self-help group
B.   clergy
C.   clinician
D.   inpatient facility

36) One of the most common criticisms of diagnosis is that it   36. _____

A.   is not a systematic process
B.   follows a medical model
C.   places meaningless labels on clients
D.   is subjective

37) For social workers in managerial positions who engage in program   37. _____
development, it is MOST important to be competent in

A.   guiding consumers in developing self-help programs
B.   organizing data in a way that increases the likelihood of gaining program support
C.   educating clients, professionals, and the community about the design
and implementation of social programs
D.   coordinating staff efforts in government-authorized service delivery
programs

38) During the social work process, clients sometimes attempt to conceal   38. _____
their weaknesses by emphasizing their more desirable traits. This is an ego
defense mechanism known as

A.   identification
B.   compensation
C.   denial
D.   rationalization

39) In attempting to paraphrase clients' statements, a practitioner should   39. _____
FIRST

A.   select an appropriate beginning or sentence stem for the paraphrase
B.   identify the emotions that are conveyed by the client's messages
C.   identify any vague or confusing parts to the message
D.   covertly restate the client's message to herself

40) The _____ model of human services organization   40. _____
management places the greatest value on maintaining stable and dependable
procedures within the organization.

A.   internal process
B.   human relations
C.   open-system
D.   rational goal

41) Which of the following is NOT one of the major categories covered in   41. _____
a mental status examination?

A.   Executive functioning
B.   Impulse control
C.   Mood and affect
D.   Level of consciousness

42) Multivariate methods of data analysis include   42. _____

      I.   factor analysis
      II.   multiple regression
      III.   descriptive statistics
      IV.   cross-tabulation

A.   I and II
B.   II only
C.   II, III and IV
D.   I, II, III and IV

43)   The human personality   43. _____

A.   appears to be organized into patterns that are observable and
measurable to some degree
B.   is a product solely of social and cultural environments, and
has no basis in biology
C.   involves unique characteristics, none of which are shared
with others
D.   is a term used to refer to the deeper core of a person, rather than super-
ficial aspects

44)   In transactional analysis, nonverbal behaviors are often used to assess   44. _____

A.   hidden and unresolved conflicts and "armoring"
B.   mixed messages
C.   ego states
D.   mistaken logic

45)   A practitioner in a small rural community is considering entering a   45. _____
dual relationship with a client—specifically, the practitioner has a flat tire and
the client owns the only tire shop in town. The practitioner should

        I.   warn the client about the potential risks of adding a business
                association to their professional relationship
        II.   accept a discounted rate for services only if it is offered by the
                client
        III.   consult with colleagues about how to handle the dual relation
                ships
        IV.   not enter into a dual relationship with the client under any cir
                cumstances

A.   I only
B.   I, II and III
C.   I and III
D.   IV only

46)   According to Erving Goffman, the function of stigma is to   46. _____

A.   reward those who conform
B.   diminish the importance of a behavior
C.   define a behavior as deviant
D.   punish a person for violating a norm

47) The Americans with Disabilities Act addresses each of the following, EXCEPT

47. _____

A. access of disabled persons to public and private facilities
B. disability benefits
C. hiring
D. accommodation of disabled persons on the job

48) A clinician is working with a client from an ethnic group that is different from her own, and is unsure about how to address the client or even what term to use to describe his community. The best practice for working with this person would be to

48. _____

A. tentatively offer the best guess and see how it is received
B. ask him what titles or labels are most comfortable for him
C. adopt the terminology that is most widely used throughout the agency
D. check the prevailing literature beforehand

49) The knowledge base of direct social work practice in health care settings is typically informed by one or more of the following models, EXCEPT the _____ model.

49. _____

A. psychiatric
B. wellness prevention and promotion
C. developmental
D. behavioral

50) Generally speaking, the standard age of consent for psychotherapy is _____ years.

50. _____

A. 14
B. 16
C. 18
D. 21

51) Ideologies provide

51. _____

I. practical guide for decision-making
II. a rationale for action
III. a way to interpret events
IV. facts

A. I and II
B. I, II and III
C. II and III
D. I, II, III and IV

52) The phase in case management during which the case manager must draw upon advanced clinical skills to assist the client in making use of services is known as

A. service implementation and coordination
B. monitoring service delivery
C. assessment and diagnosis
D. advocacy

53) During an assessment interview, a practitioner asks a client: "Is there anything going on with you physically—the way you eat, smoke, or sleep, for example—that affects or leads to this problem?" The practitioner is trying to identify _____ antecedents to the client's problem.

A. behavioral
B. affective
C. somatic
D. contextual

54) Ethically, a clinician should

A. inform a client that a diagnosis can become a permanent part of a file and have ramifications in terms of insurance costs and employment
B. inform clients that their records are the property of the clinician or the agency
C. be willing to alter case notes if they will prove damaging to a client's case in court
D. be available to vulnerable clients 24 hours a day

55) Because of the social stigma attached to mental illness by many Asian Americans, it is important that services be

A. delivered by traditional helpers within the community
B. educational and matter-of-fact
C. presented in language that refers to the spiritual or religious
D. disguised as social gatherings

56) Clinical social workers so NOT typically consult with

A. administrators
B. other professionals in different fields who are working with the same clients
C. other mental health professionals about legal issues
D. other mental health professionals about clinical decisions

57)   In clinical practice, "obsessions" refer to

A.   psychoses
B.   behaviors
C.   ritualistic patterns
D.   thoughts

58)   When a client tries to resist compliance with a suggestion or treatment
by manipulating the image of the person making the recommendation (the
clinician), the client is engaging in

A.   identity management
B.   altercasting
C.   negotiation
D.   non-negotiation

59)   Strategic planning within a human services organization

A.   must be tailored to the organization's planning culture
B.   by its nature, affects volunteers but does not involve them in the pro-
cess
C.   is an undertaking limited to top management
D.   generally requires more time than money

60)   In Maslow's model, high levels of a fear of success are correlated with
high

A.   affective habituation
B.   fear of failure
C.   extrinsic motivation
D.   self-esteem

61)   A popular assessment tool for determining the degree of a person's
intent to harm him/herself divide indicators into Level 1 through Level 4, with
Level 4 being the most urgent and probably requiring hospitalization. Which
of the following would be considered a Level 4 indicator?

A.   Occasional suicidal ideation, but without behavioral indicators of in-
tent
B.   An acute episode of mental health illness requiring new medication
C.   A moderate impairment in social and occupational functioning
D.   An inability to control of the stability of one's behavior, with or with-
out a supportive social environment

62)   Because social workers are increasingly called upon to coordinate   62. _____
services on behalf of clients, human service organizations are encouraged to
develop

A.   case management services
B.   horizontal affiliations
C.   systems-of-care models
D.   vertical integration

63)   In Gestalt therapy, _____ occurs when a client at-   63. _____
tributes a characteristic to the outside world that truly belongs to himself.

A.   confluence
B.   retroflection
C.   projection
D.   deflection

64)   When working with a client who is encountering serious economic   64. _____
need, the most valuable task a practitioner can perform is to

A.   help the client find a paying job
B.   verify that the client is deserving of benefits
C.   give accurate information about benefits and ensure entitlement
D.   advocate and obtain benefits for the client

65)   Which of the following is NOT a component of the therapeutic rela-   65. _____
tionship?

A.   Teaching/instructing
B.   Transference/countertransference
C.   Therapeutic alliance
D.   Collaboration

66)   The ethical principle of _____ refers to a practitioner's   66. _____
acceptance of the responsibility to promote what is good for others.

A.   nonmaleficence
B.   justice
C.   beneficence
D.   autonomy

67) According to Kohlberg's theory of moral development, a child who is greatly concerned about pleasing his parents and teachers is at the _____ _____ level of development.

    67. _____

A.   conventional
B.   pre-moral
C.   pre-conventional
D.   post-moral

68) The "Socratic method" is proposed by some as a technique for social work supervision. Which of the following is NOT an element of the Socratic method?

    68. _____

A.   Systematic questioning
B.   Inductive reasoning
C.   Utilitarian ethics
D.   Universal definitions

69) Which of the following is NOT one of the basic concepts of psychosocial therapy?

    69. _____

A.   Recognition of the unconscious
B.   Recognition of the nature of pathology
C.   A skeptical perception of the human potential
D.   Focusing on everyday living

70) A client has been released from an inpatient program for the mentally ill, but must be maintained with medication and talk therapy. Most likely, the client will make use of

    70. _____

A.   the local mental health center
B.   the hospital emergency room
C.   a private clinician
D.   a psychiatric nurse practitioner

71) Research suggests that homosexuality is best understood in terms of

    71. _____

A.   intrapsychic disposition
B.   identity formation
C.   specific genetic factors
D.   childhood sexual experience

72) The increased demand for social workers to do formal diagnosis of mental disorders has been influenced by several factors. Which of the following is NOT one of these factors?

72. _____

A. Nearly half of all Americans will have a significant mental illness in their lifetimes.
B. Nonmedical professionals are increasingly required to serve the mentally ill as mental health services are decreased.
C. Payers for services require a diagnosis before authorizing or reimbursing for mental health services.
D. Generally, knowledge of the *DSM-IV* is limited to clinical professionals.

73) Which of the following is NOT an advantage associated with private practice social work?

73. _____

A. Greater consumer choice among service providers
B. More manageable paperwork and meeting requirements
C. Fewer incidences of conflict-of-interest situations
D. Fewer organizational constraints

74) The Bowen family systems theory centers on the counterbalancing life forces of

74. _____

A. togetherness and individuality
B. nature and nurturance
C. cohesiveness and adaptability
D. conflict and harmony

75) A clinician is working with a family in conflict. To the mother, the conflict is about the quality of interactions within the family and managing interpersonal tension and hostility. In other words, the mother sees it as a(n) _____ conflict.

75. _____

A. pseudo-
B. ego
C. expressive
D. instrumental

KEY (CORRECT ANSWERS)

1.	A	41.	A
2.	A	42.	A
3.	A	43.	A
4.	B	44.	C
5.	D	45.	C
6.	D	46.	C
7.	D	47.	B
8.	A	48.	B
9.	B	49.	D
10.	C	50.	C
11.	B	51.	C
12.	B	52.	A
13.	B	53.	C
14.	C	54.	A
15.	B	55.	B
16.	C	56.	C
17.	B	57.	D
18.	A	58.	A
19.	A	59.	A
20.	A	60.	D
21.	B	61.	D
22.	D	62.	B
23.	D	63.	C
24.	C	64.	C
25.	C	65.	A
26.	A	66.	C
27.	A	67.	A
28.	D	68.	C
29.	C	69.	C
30.	D	70.	A
31.	C	71.	B
32.	A	72.	D
33.	D	73.	C
34.	B	74.	A
35.	A	75.	C
36.	C		
37.	B		
38.	B		
39.	D		
40.	A		

EXAMINATION SECTION
TEST 1

DIRECTIONS: Each question or incomplete statement is followed by several suggested answers or completions. Select the one that BEST answers the question or completes the statement. *PRINT THE LETTER OF THE CORRECT ANSWER IN THE SPACE AT THE RIGHT.*

Questions 1-6.

DIRECTIONS: Questions 1 through 6 are to be answered on the basis of the following information.

The nursing staff on a medical unit meets every week to discuss problem areas they are encountering while giving nursing care. The areas of discussion are (1) the nursing process and (2) emotional needs of clients.

1. The first staff meeting covers the best nursing approach to meet the clients' emotional needs.
   Which basic factor should be determined FIRST by the staff?
   A. Why the clients behave as they do
   B. Which nursing approach has been effective or needs changing
   C. Which clients have symptoms of increased anxiety
   D. What dependent needs of the client the nurse can meet   1.___

2. The staff discusses methods of data collection by the nurse.
   Which would be the MOST significant in making a nursing care plan?
   A. The nursing report on the client's problems
   B. The physical/emotional history supplied by the client's family
   C. Reviewing the client's chart
   D. Interviewing the client immediately on admission   2.___

3. The staff agrees that the BASIC principle of planning nursing care is to
   A. accept the client as he or she is
   B. meet the client's needs
   C. believe the client will improve
   D. know the client as a person   3.___

4. The staff also stresses that, at the initial interview with the client, the nurse should use open-ended questions to collect data.
   Which question would be a good example?
   A. Are there any questions you want to ask?
   B. Tell me something about yourself.
   C. Can you give me any information?
   D. Were you brought to the hospital by your family?   4.___

5. The nursing staff discusses evaluation of nursing care.   5.__
   Which evaluation should be identified as a *halo* evaluation?
   The client('s)
   A. has learned some control
   B. behavior is to demand attention
   C. continues to be negative
   D. care plan has been effective

6. The staff identifies the best time for the nurse to record   6.__
   the observed behavior of a client.
   That time is
   A. when the behavior has become a problem
   B. at the end of every shift
   C. immediately after contact with the client
   D. after conferring with other staff members

7. Many people with mental disorders have poor self-images,   7.__
   which they need to improve in order to recover.
   All of the following factors contribute to self-image
   EXCEPT
   A. body image
   B. personally judging others
   C. relationships within the family
   D. interpersonal relationships outside of the family

8. The MOST important feeling for the nurse to convey to the   8.__
   client in order for the client to accept the nurse is one
   of
   A. respect for the client   B. willingness to help
   C. professional competence   D. no-nonsense demands

9. A patient being treated for an aggressive personality   9.__
   disorder insists that the last time he was in the clinic
   he was given lithium, which helped him, and he demands
   that the nurse get him some immediately.
   The nurse's BEST reply to this demand would be:
   A. We never administer drugs to people in your condition
   B. I will go get some for you if you calm down
   C. You don't need lithium
   D. Be patient, and I'll talk to your doctor about whether
      lithium would be appropriate for you

10. All of the following principles of psychiatric-mental   10.__
    health nursing help form the basis of the therapeutic
    use of self EXCEPT:
    A. Be aware of your own feelings and responses and main-
       tain objectivity while being aware of your own needs
    B. Accept clients as they are, be nonjudgmental, and
       recognize that emotions influence behaviors
    C. Use sympathy, not empathy, and observe a client's
       behaviors to analyze needs and problems
    D. Avoid verbal reprimands, physical force, giving
       advice, or imposing your own values on clients.
       Also assess clients in the context of their social
       and cultural group.

Questions 11-20.

DIRECTIONS: Questions 11 through 20 are to be answered on the
basis of the following information.

Pete Jones, the mental health nurse specialist, conducts group
therapy sessions for the outpatient clinic.

11. During group formation, Mr. Jones should SPECIFICALLY   11.___
     select a group of clients that is no more than _____ in
     number and has homogeneity of _____.
        A. 6; goals
        B. 4; age and sex
        C. 14; ability and willingness
        D. 10; problems and needs

12. Mr. Jones has selected his group, and they meet daily from   12.___
     2 to 3 P.M. It is a closed group and does not allow any
     interruptions.
     During the period that it takes the group to become
     acquainted, what kind of behavior would Mr. Jones expect
     from the group?
        A. Open and positive interaction, rather than projection
           of their feelings
        B. Conflict, lack of unity, testing, and politeness
           toward each other
        C. Trust and acceptance of each other and the therapist
        D. Discussion centering on the mental health unit and
           their expectations

13. Mr. Jones explains to the group that its main function is   13.___
     sharing feelings and behaviors among the members. The
     group is often a substitute for, or is compared to, one's
     own family.
     What does the group accomplish for each member through
     this identification process?
     The group
        A. gives the client hope in himself and makes him
           realize that others are available for comfort and
           acceptance
        B. teaches the client new skills in socialization that
           will be more acceptable to his family
        C. assists the client in replacing negative past
           experiences with a new set of positive group experi-
           ences
        D. helps the client feel that he is being helpful and
           interested in the well-being of others

14. Mr. Jones' group therapy is based on interventive-explora-   14.___
     tory therapy.
     When he defines this type of therapy to his group, what
     should he say?
        A. You will verbally express your emotional problems
           with individual and group relationships.

B. The main focus of this group is the support of existing coping mechanisms.
C. The emphasis is on social interaction, which encourages control.
D. This is an intellectual and emotional exchange of things that you value.

15. Mr. Jones observes that one of the clients monopolizes the group discussion.
What action should Mr. Jones take?
A. Accept the client's behavior as his/her way of coping
B. Allow the group members to intervene if they are able to
C. Interrupt and ask the client to limit the discussion
D. Ask another client if this discussion is relevant

16. One of the clients in the group is verbally aggressive toward another client.
What should Mr. Jones do INITIALLY?
A. Set up individual therapy to explore the hostile client's feelings
B. Ask the aggressive client to leave the group until control is gained
C. Set an example by being uninvolved with the aggressor
D. Sit still, observe, and avoid taking sides with either client

17. Mr. Jones and the group feel that they are not progressing.
What should the group do?
A. Explore the reasons for the lack of group productivity
B. Establish other goals that will be more compatible to the group
C. Disband because the members are not compatible
D. Accept new members into the group to provide more feedback

18. After a group session, one of the clients says, *Today I felt we were really a group.*
When Mr. Jones asks that client to identify the reason for this feeling, which response demonstrates ACCURATELY that the group was cohesive?
A. We have learned to speak directly to each other rather than to the whole group.
B. We have been able to discuss similarities of thoughts and conflicts.
C. We have not been so hostile or anxious with each other.
D. As individuals, each one has identified ways of fulfilling his or her goal.

19. During one of the group sessions, Mrs. Elena tells Mr. Jones that he is one of the smartest men she has ever known and feels she has learned so much from him.
How should Mr. Jones respond?

A. That is very nice of you, but we are not here to discuss me.
B. We are not here to give compliments to any one member.
C. You seem anxious, share your feelings with us.
D. The purpose of the group is to learn more about each other.

20. The group has reached its goal and is now talking about termination.
Which action by the group members shows that they are ready to terminate the group?
A. Members no longer feel abandoned, rejected, or forsaken.
B. Feelings are expressed that members of the group will keep in touch.
C. Each member learns to handle his or her own feelings of loss without support.
D. There is effective coping with feelings of loss and separation anxiety.

20.___

KEY (CORRECT ANSWERS)

1. C
2. D
3. A
4. B
5. C

6. C
7. B
8. A
9. D
10. C

11. D
12. B
13. C
14. A
15. B

16. D
17. A
18. B
19. C
20. D

TEST 2

DIRECTIONS: Each question or incomplete statement is followed by several suggested answers or completions. Select the one that BEST answers the question or completes the statement. *PRINT THE LETTER OF THE CORRECT ANSWER IN THE SPACE AT THE RIGHT.*

Questions 1-6.

DIRECTIONS: Questions 1 through 6 are to be answered on the basis of the following information.

Ms. Cohen is a nurse working in a crisis center with a volunteer group.

1. One of the volunteers asks, *What is a crisis?* 1.___
   The nurse should reply that a crisis is a situation in which the person or family
   A. is too subjectively involved to realize when there is a problem
   B. constantly looks to others to resolve certain conflicts
   C. has difficulty with growth and development periods
   D. has had no experience in knowing how to deal with a problem

2. Ms. Cohen tells the volunteers that those working with 2.___
   people in crisis should recognize that one of the first reactions to crisis is the use of defense mechanisms. They should know that these defenses at the time of a crisis
   A. are useful in helping clients protect themselves
   B. are irrelevant, as they are part of the basic personality
   C. should be interrupted to prevent further damage
   D. are an indication that the client is coping well

3. Ms. Cohen explains to the group that people in crisis often 3.___
   use isolation as a defense. Ms. Cohen asks, *Which behavior should be assessed as isolation?*
   The person
   A. blames others for causing the problem
   B. minimizes the seriousness of the problem
   C. accepts the problem intellectually but not emotionally
   D. puts excess energy in another area to neutralize the problem

4. Ms. Cohen instructs the volunteers that when people in 4.___
   crisis first come to the center to seek information about their problem, only specific questions should be answered, with no details given at this time.
   Why is this approach taken?

    A. The person may be mentally incompetent and may lose
       control.
    B. A nurse or doctor should give specific information.
    C. The person may be overwhelmed with excessive infor-
       mation.
    D. The person is not interested in detailed information.

5. Ms. Cohen states that when a person is in crisis, the   5.___
    BEST support group would be
       A. the volunteers in the community
       B. close family and friends understanding the problem
       C. other people who have similar problems
       D. the professional working in the crisis center

6. One of the volunteers asks, *Why is the crisis intervention*   6.___
    limited from 1 to 6 weeks?
    Ms. Cohen replies that a person can stand the disequili-
    brium only for a limited time, and during this time will
       A. more likely accept intervention to help with coping
       B. return to a familiar pattern of behavior
       C. require long-term counseling after this period
       D. refuse help from any other support group

Questions 7-11.

DIRECTIONS: Questions 7 through 11 are to be answered on the
              basis of the following information.

    Lauren Oland, age 14, was brought to the crisis center by a
policeman. She had been raped by a friend of the family.

7. Which nursing action should have TOP priority?   7.___
       A. Explain to her that she will be safe here.
       B. Get a detailed description of the attack.
       C. Have a calm and accepting approach.
       D. Treat her physical wounds.

8. Lauren Oland sobs, *My family will kill me if they find out.* 8.___
    Which response by the nurse would be MOST appropriate?
       A. You are underage so your family will have to be
          informed.
       B. Your family is your best support at this time.
       C. Don't you think that they would rather kill the man?
       D. Tell me how your family reacts during stressful times.

9. After Lauren calms down and accepts Ms. Cohen, she con-   9.___
    fides, *I feel so dirty. I will never feel clean again.*
    How should the nurse reply?
       A. This is a normal feeling after what has happened to
          you.
       B. Are you saying you feel guilty? Let's talk about
          that feeling.
       C. I can understand; I would feel the same way.
       D. You shouldn't think of yourself as dirty; it wasn't
          your fault.

10. Lauren tells the nurse, *I feel like my love life is over.* 10.__
No decent boy will ever look at me again.
To help Lauren assess the situation, how should the nurse
reply?
    A. I know it is difficult, but you are strong.
    B. You are not to blame so you shouldn't punish yourself.
    C. What was your relationship with boys before?
    D. You are a pretty girl; you will have many boyfriends.

11. Lauren tells Ms. Cohen that she will not testify against 11.__
the family friend because then everyone will know about
her.
Which reply by the nurse would BEST help Lauren with this
plan of action?
    A. How do you think you will feel if you do nothing?
    B. It will be a closed court, so no one will know.
    C. This is difficult, but I'm sure you will make the
       right choice.
    D. You have an obligation to protect other women from
       this man.

Questions 12-15.

DIRECTIONS: Questions 12 through 15 are to be answered on the
basis of the following information.

    Kirt Russel, a volunteer, answers the hotline. The caller, a
female, tells Kirt that she plans on killing herself.

12. How should Kirt reply? 12.__
    A. Are you alone? Is there someone else that I can
       talk to?
    B. How do you plan on killing yourself?
    C. You have called the right number to prevent that from
       happening.
    D. What is your name, address, and telephone number?

13. What is the BEST approach for Kirt to take while talking 13.__
to the *suicide caller*?
    A. Neutral, not condoning or condemning
    B. Distracting the caller from talking about suicide
    C. One of concern and support
    D. Acting as the conscience of the caller

14. The caller identifies herself as Barbra and states that 14.__
she is going to poison herself.
What should Kirt then say?
    A. Have you thought of the agony of such a death?
    B. What kind of poison are you going to take?
    C. Tell me if you've ever had these feelings before.
    D. Give me the name of your doctor.

15. Kirt keeps Barbra on the phone, pleading with her not to   15.___
    hang up, but to keep talking to him.
    Kirt's purpose in doing this is to
        A. give her time to gain her equilibrium and reconsider
           her actions
        B. let her know that someone cares enough to talk to her
        C. keep her mind off her problems and the thought of
           suicide
        D. keep her occupied until an emergency team arrives

Questions 16-20.

DIRECTIONS: Questions 16 through 20 are to be answered on the
             basis of the following information.

    Doreen Darby is a 16 year-old high school student with a history
of poor social contact. Always an introvert, for the past month
Doreen has refused to go to school, spent her time in bed, and taken
nourishment only when spoon-fed. Her family took her to the
emergency room of the general hospital when she reported that voices
had told her she was *no good and should stay away from others.*

16. The nurse in the emergency room identifies Doreen's   16.___
    behavior as depersonalization.
    This term is BEST described as
        A. pathological narcissism
        B. inability to empathize with others
        C. experiencing the world as dreamlike
        D. absence of a moral code

17. The staff is planning Doreen's immediate care.   17.___
    The MOST suitable choice at this time would be
        A. weekly visits to the psychiatric clinic for medical
           therapy and psychotherapy
        B. a small psychiatric unit for 24 hour-a-day treatment
        C. attendance at the day hospital and home with her
           family at night
        D. in her home, with her family, under the supervision
           of a psychiatrist

18. Doreen is assessed as having low self-esteem.   18.___
    Which characteristic BEST defines this problem?
        A. Social withdrawal   B. Flat faces
        C. Alienation from self   D. Feelings of persecution

19. The nursing staff plans an intensive therapeutic approach   19.___
    for Doreen.
    Such an approach is CRUCIAL for Doreen because
        A. she will be missing her family, which is her primary
           support group
        B. she is acutely ill and is completely out of contact
           with reality

C. the staff must thoroughly evaluate Doreen's physical,
social, and emotional condition
D. it is critical for her to learn to trust those in her
environment

20. Doreen has learned to relate to her primary nurse but
refuses to get involved in any of the activities with
others on the unit.
Which approach by her primary nurse would be the MOST
therapeutic for Doreen?
A. Telling Doreen she is expected at assigned activities
B. Becoming involved in activities with Doreen
C. Observing Doreen with others
D. Waiting until Doreen asks to attend the activities

Questions 21-25.

DIRECTIONS: Questions 21 through 25 are to be answered on the
basis of the following information.

Mrs. Agnes Smith comes to the crisis center with her two small
daughters, ages 3 and 4. She has numerous contusions on her face
and body. She tells the nurse, *I've been beaten by my husband for
the last time. I want to leave him but have no place to go. Maybe
when he sobers up, I can go back - if he will go on the wagon.*

21. Which analysis by the nurse takes PRIORITY?
A. Recognize that the client is correct in wanting to
leave her husband
B. Know the effect the problem will have on the client
C. Use own past experience to help the client understand
her problem
D. Understand the implications of the problem from the
client's viewpoint

22. During the assessment period, which question should the
nurse ask Mrs. Smith?
A. Why can't you plan to live with your family?
B. Does your husband earn enough to support two house-
holds?
C. How often does your husband beat you?
D. You say you want to go yet stay. Are there any
alternatives we can discuss?

23. Mrs. Smith has identified her problem as being too
dependent on her husband.
What plan would BEST help her resolve this problem?
A. Learn to have a better self-image
B. Talk to her husband about her need to be independent
C. Find a new home for herself and her children
D. Go to school or get a job

24. The children and Mrs. Smith have made contact with friends   24.___
    and will be temporarily staying with them.
    The nurse understands that this is important for the family
    at this time because
        A. the tension in their own home is too great
        B. in a neutral environment Mrs. Smith can better plan
           for the future
        C. they will be safer there than in their own home
        D. both the abuser and abused need time apart

25. Mrs. Smith plans to go to group therapy.   25.___
    Which group would be MOST beneficial at this time?
        A. Abusers Anonymous
        B. Family therapy
        C. Parents without partners
        D. Al-Anon

KEY (CORRECT ANSWERS)

1. D			11. A	
2. A			12. D	
3. C			13. C	
4. C			14. B	
5. B			15. D	
6. A			16. C	
7. C			17. B	
8. D			18. A	
9. B			19. D	
10. C			20. B	

21. D
22. D
23. A
24. C
25. B

EXAMINATION SECTION
TEST 1

Directions: Each question or incomplete statement is followed by several suggested answers or completions. Select the one the BEST answers the question or completes the statement. *PRINT THE LETTER OF THE CORRECT ANSWER IN THE SPACE AT THE RIGHT.*

1) Each of the following is a risk factor that is associated with a greater likelihood for intimate partner violence, EXCEPT

A. women aged 39 to 49
B. stalking
C. alcohol or drug abuse
D. families with low incomes

1. _____

2) In abusive domestic relationships, a woman's risk of homicide is typically greatest

A. when she is living with the man
B. when children are not present
C. in the first two months of any separation
D. immediately following an instance of acute battering

2. _____

3) The historical standard of a sexual assault victim fighting her attacker and demonstrating the "utmost resistance" is an example of:

A. victim precipitation
B. victim provocation
C. lack of victim consent
D. offender *mens rea*

3. _____

4) A woman is not yet ready to leave her abusive husband because she is unsure of how she will support her son, whom she intends to take with her when she does leave. The woman works with a domestic violence professional on a safety plan for her son to follow. This plan should include each of the following elements, EXCEPT

A. find a safe place to retreat to during a battering episode.
B. call 911 if you think somebody in the family might get hurt.
C. if you don't approve of the abuser's behavior during an episode, tell him so.
D. find a person you can trust to talk to about what is going on at home and how you feel about it

4. _____

5)   For a domestic violence professional, the process of assessment ends   5. _____
when

A.   the last assessment interview or form has been recorded
B.   a safety plan has been formulated
C.   the first set of behavioral and/or environmental goals are met
D.   the terminal phase of service is complete

6)   "Victim precipitation" refers to the idea that the   6. _____

A.   offender carefully selects victims with certain characteristics
B.   offender lacks a *mens rea*, or criminal intent
C.   victim somehow caused his or her own victimization
D.   victim should be the prime instigator of criminal prosecution

7)   In cases of domestic violence, research suggests that criminal justice   7. _____
interventions are most effective at reducing the chances of reassault by perpetrators who

A.   use the "loss of control" explanation for their attacks
B.   commit less severe violence
C.   are arrested as a result of a victim-initiated complaint
D.   commit sexual violence as part of their abusive behavior

8)   "Permanency planning" refers to the policy of

A.   developing a stable foster care plan for children removed from their   8. _____
homes
B.   assuring abused and neglected children a stable family situation
throughout childhood
C.   using adoption for at-risk children
D.   interventions for children who are at risk of removal, or who have
been removed from, their homes

9)   The National Domestic Violence Hotline is a program of the U.S.   9. _____

A.   Department of Health and Human Services
B.   Department of Housing and Urban Development
C.   Department of Justice
D.   Occupational Health and Safety Administration

10)   Which of the following is NOT a privileged relationship during the
prosecution of child abuse?

10. _____

A.   Priest-penitent
B.   Lawyer-client
C.   Psychologist-patient
D.   Doctor-patient

11)   A domestic violence professional begins an investigation of a report by
visiting the home of a family and observing that a child has several bruises on
her back, arms, and legs. In order to maintain professional objectivity, the
worker should describe the child as

11. _____

A.   self-destructive
B.   clumsy
C.   abused
D.   bruised

12)   Generally, the odds of criminal victimization for the elderly are:

12. _____

A.   about the same as other age groups
B.   slightly higher than other age groups
C.   lower than other age groups
D.   markedly higher than other age groups

13)   The most prevalent form of elder maltreatment is

13. _____

A.   physical abuse
B.   active neglect
C.   material abuse
D.   self-neglect

14)   A domestic violence professional is unable to convince a victim of
domestic violence to leave her situation. The professional should advise the
victim to

14. _____

    I.   fight back when the behavior begins, to make violence more
            difficult
    II.   stay away from children during an abusive episode
    III.   purchase a defensive device such as mace or a "stun gun" in
            case the violence escalates to a level that is life-threatening
    IV.   conceal the abuse as much as possible from family and friends

A.   I and III
B.   II only
C.   None of the above
D.   All of the above

15)   Which of the following is LEAST likely to be a sign or symptom of   15. _____
elder abuse?

A.   bone fractures
B.   elder's sudden change in behavior
C.   elder reports of abuse
D.   untreated health problems

16)   Physical discipline by a parent is permitted in all states, provided it is   16. _____
reasonable and not excessive. The "reasonableness" standard is largely
dependent on

A.   the size of the child
B.   whether the child is seriously hurt
C.   the culture in which the parent was raised
D.   the age of the child

17)   The most common form of rape is described as _____ rape.   17. _____

A.   stranger
B.   acquaintance
C.   sadistic
D.   spousal

18)   Conflicts between two pieces of federal legislation, the Adoption
Assistance and Child Welfare Act of 1980 and the Child Abuse Prevention and   18. _____
Treatment Act of 1974, center on the issue of

A.   what constitutes "abuse"
B.   whether details of a child's history of abuse should be revealed to
parents who are candidates for adoption
C.   whether it's best for a child to remain in or be removed from an abu-
sive situation
D.   what constitutes "neglect"

19)   An order of protection is issued in New York, and afterwards the   19. _____
girlfriend of an abuser moves onto the Pine Ridge Indian Reservation in South
Dakota. The abuser tracks her down, enters the reservation, and begins to
harass the woman at her new home. Tribal law determines each of the following, EXCEPT

A.   the arrest authority of responding law enforcement
B.   how long the order is in effect
C.   detention and notification procedures
D.   penalties and sanctions for violations of the order

20) The _____ was instrumental in establishing policy guidelines for handling spouse abuse incidents

20. _____

A.   Zimbardo experiment
B.   Minneapolis experiment
C.   President's Task Force on Family Violence
D.   President's Task Force on Victims of Crime

21) A woman has left her abusive boyfriend and wants to get her and her children's names legally changed, in order to make it more difficult to find them. The boyfriend is the father of the children. The main difficulty she will have in doing this is that

21. _____

A.   the father must be notified of the children's name changes
B.   agencies and creditors are unlikely to recognize the children's new names along with her own
C.   the father will automatically be notified of the children's new names
D.   legally, the children's names cannot be changed

22) Women who have been beaten repeatedly over a period of many years often suffer from "battering syndrome" or "battered women's syndrome." Women who exhibit this syndrome share the essential characteristics of

22. _____

I.   alcohol and/or substance abuse
II.   debilitating fear of physical aggression
III.   unpredictable displays of physical aggression
IV.   flashbacks

A.   I and II
B.   II and III
C.   III only
D.   I, II, III and IV

23) Battered women's shelters are typically funded through each of the following, EXCEPT

23. _____

A.   grants from organizations like the United Way
B.   marriage license fees
C.   private donations
D.   victim compensation payouts

24)   When a woman leaves an abuser, the abuser goes through a predictable   24. _____
process of emotions known as the "separation cycle." The first phase of this
process is usually

A.   manipulative anger
B.   defaming the survivor to others
C.   indifference
D.   manipulative courting

25)   Under the Violence Against Women Act, an order of protection is   25. _____
universally valid if it meets certain minimal requirements. These include

    I.   it cannot be issued *ex parte*
    II.   the court that issued the order must have personal jurisdiction
            over the parties and subject matter jurisdiction over the case
    III.   the respondent must have had notice and an opportunity to be
            heard
    IV.   the order must be a criminal, rather than civil, order

A.   I only
B.   I and II
C.   II and III
D.   III and IV

KEY (CORRECT ANSWERS)

1. A
2. C
3. C
4. C
5. D

6. C
7. B
8. B
9. A
10. D

11. D
12. C
13. D
14. B
15. D

16. B
17. B
18. C
19. B
20. B

21. A
22. B
23. D
24. C
25. C

TEST 2

Directions: Each question or incomplete statement is followed by several suggested answers or completions. Select the one the BEST answers the question or completes the statement. *PRINT THE LETTER OF THE CORRECT ANSWER IN THE SPACE AT THE RIGHT.*

1) Professionals who are working with clients who are in an abusive relationship should try to communicate that

1. _____

A. leaving the abusive situation is always the safest solution
B. usually, waiting to effect a mutual end to the relationship is the only lasting solution
C. only the abused person can ultimately judge what will be the safest option
D. ending an abusive relationship requires behavior changes from both partners

2) Violence between _____ would typically NOT be covered under a domestic violence statute.

2. _____

A. two cohabiting homosexual lovers
B. siblings
C. grandfather and grandson
D. two roommates

3) Goals of advocacy for victims of domestic violence include

3. _____

I. increasing victims' ability to make a successful transition to independence
II. empowering women to make significant changes and solve problems
III. connecting the victim with community resources, both short- and long-term
IV. insuring the prosecution and punishment of the batterer

A. II and III
B. I, II, and III
C. II, III, and IV
D. All of the above

=

4) Which of the following is NOT a theoretical explanation for elder abuse and neglect?   4. _____

A. Situational transaction
B. Role reversal
C. Violent subculture
D. Social exchange

5) The Wellstone/Murray amendment to the Personal Responsibility and Work Opportunity Reconciliation Act (PRWORA—commonly known as the Welfare Reform Act) means that victims of domestic violence   5. _____

A. may receive welfare benefits only if they take active steps to end an abusive situation, such as taking up residence at a shelter
B. may not have to meet the work requirements and time limits that apply to other welfare recipients
C. must receive psycho-educational group counseling in order to receive benefits
D. are qualified for any state-funded intervention program

6) Which of the following terms is synonymous with "repeat victimiza-tion"?   6. _____

A. Multiple offenders victimizing a single individual
B. Offender recidivism
C. Victim recidivism
D. A single offender with multiple victims

7) Which of the following variables is a vulnerability factor for the elderly?   7. _____

A. Living alone or with someone
B. Residential location
C. Amount of fear of crime
D. Degree of social support

8) A young wife visits a domestic violence professional and reports that she is extremely unhappy. She report numerous episodes of domestic vio-lence, and asks the professional whether the marriage is worth saving. The professional should   8. _____

A. recommend divorce, given the domestic violence
B. tell the woman that a divorce is their decision alone
C. advise a trial separation
D. contact the police about the domestic violence

9) In most states, professionals who are required to report the possibility 9. _____
of child maltreatment to the proper authority include

      I.   police officers
      II.   domestic violence professionals
      III.   medical or hospital personnel
      IV.   attorneys

A.   I and II
B.   I, II and III
C.   III only
D.   I, II, III and IV

10) In a family, which is a "low" risk factor for child abuse or neglect? 10. _____

A.   Only child
B.   Limited physical and mental abilities of child
C.   Single parent
D.   Younger child

11) The government may intervene in cases of elder abuse if the 11. _____

      I.   older person requests it
      II.   older person is found at a hearing to be incompetent
      III.   abuse or neglect presents an unacceptable level of danger to the
             older person
      IV.   abuse is properly reported and recorded by a visiting social
             services worker

A.   I only
B.   I and II
C.   I, II and III
D.   I, II, III and IV

12) For the survivor of abuse, the full faith and credit provisions of the 12. _____
Violence Against Women Act mean that

A.   they can call on law enforcement officers anywhere in the United
States to enforce orders of protection across state or tribal lines
B.   they can apply for orders of protection in different and unlimited
jurisdictions if they decide to move across state lines
C.   if a victim's claim of domestic abuse has upheld by the law once, all
subsequent claims against the same perpetrator will be assumed to be factual
unless proven otherwise
D.   they will be eligible for certain services administered by the Department of Justice

13)   Two months ago, not long after her husband assaulted her badly   13. _____
enough to break her arm, a woman moved into a shelter for battered women.
The husband is alcoholic and has been abusive for as long as they've been
married, about six years. The woman tells a domestic violence professional
that she has decided to return to her husband in an attempt to save her marriage. The professional should

A.   discuss the possible consequences of returning to her spouse as compared to remaining in the shelter, but let her make her own choice
B.   strongly advise the woman to remain in the shelter, using statistics that
support the contention that she will likely be abused again if she returns home
C.   tell the woman that if returning to her husband is her wish, then she
should return to her spouse.
D.   tell her that she should think of the welfare of her children before she
decides to return to an abusive household

14)   Provisions of the Violence Against Women Act include each of the   14. _____
following, EXCEPT

A.   prioritization of home state jurisdictions over others in the enforcement of child custody orders
B.   prohibiting anyone facing a domestic violence protection order from
possessing a firearm
C.   establishment of crossing state lines to continue the abuse of a spouse
or partner as a federal crime
D.   requiring sexual offenders to pay restitution to their victims

15)   Which of the following variables would MOST likely be classified as   15. _____
constituting a high risk for either domestic violence or child abuse?

A.   A recent change in marital or relationship status
B.   Water and/or electricity inoperative
C.   A child between 5 and 9 years of age
D.   Family does not belong to a church or social group

16)   As of 2003, there were seven U.S. states in which domestic violence   16. _____
protection orders were explicitly unavailable for victims of same-sex abuse.
Which of the following is one of these states?

A.   Texas
B.   Illinois
C.   Wyoming
D.   New York

17)   A battered wife has decided to take a case against her husband to   17. _____
Family Court. Which of the following is a DISADVANTAGE associated with
the prosecution of domestic violence offenses in Family Court?

A.   It is more difficult to receive a Temporary Order of Protection from
Family Court.
B.   The only thing an Order of Protection issued by a Family Court can do
is prevent the abuser from causing physical harm.
C.   An Order of Protection issued by a Family Court cannot be automati-
cally extended once it expires.
D.   A Family Court judge cannot put an abuser in jail even if the abuser
admits to doing the things involved in the petition.

18)   Which of the following is a guideline for domestic violence victim   18. _____
validation?

A.   Downplay the widespread prevalence of such crimes among all
women
B.   Avoid speaking directly about the violence
C.   Stress the criminal nature of the violence and the fact that the victim is
not to blame
D.   Seek verification of the victim's story from second parties

19)   Child abuse generally does NOT refer to   19. _____

A.   withholding of life's essentials
B.   nonaccidental infliction of injury
C.   fondling a child
D.   pornography

20)   A woman is working with a domestic violence professional on a   20. _____
written personalized safety plan. The FIRST element of such a plan should
typically focus on

A.   the procedures for obtaining a protection order
B.   safety when preparing to leave
C.   a checklist of items to take when leaving
D.   safety during a violent incident

21) A woman fears that if she stays with her husband, the Child Protective   21. _____
Services agency may attempt to take her children, who are also being abused,
out of the home. The domestic violence professional should be aware that
such decisions are based on two issues. These are

       I.   the motivation, capacity for harm, and intent of the alleged
                  abuser
       II.   whether the domestic violence victim has a plan for leaving the
                  abuser in place and is ready to act on it
       III.   the natural support network available to the mother and chil
                  dren.
       IV.   the immediate danger or risk to the child

A.   I and IV
B.   II and III
C.   II and IV
D.   III and IV

22) An injunction in a spouse abuse situation may NOT be characterized   22. _____
by

A.   issuance on an *ex parte* basis
B.   having same effect as a trespass warning
C.   a filing fee waiver
D.   a status equivalent to that of divorce

23) Orders of protection against abusers often include terms that award   23. _____
custody of the minor children to the victim. Advocates for domestic violence
victims should be aware that these custody provisions

A.   are not specifically enforceable if the victim takes the children across
the state line
B.   are subject to the provisions of the Violence Against Women Act
C.   must be petitioned and filed separately for each child
D.   must be agreed to by the children's father

24)   A woman comes to a domestic violence professional seeking help. 24. _____
She has been involved with a batterer for more than a year now, and the
beatings are getting progressively worse—recently, blackening an eye so
severely that she was forced to stay home from work. Strangely, this was not
the event that drove the woman to seek help. What frightens the woman most
is that she hardly recalls the last few episodes. She doesn't remember feeling
any fear or pain while she was being assaulted, she says; she felt numb,
mostly, and actually thought about the things she still had left to do on that
day as she was being beaten. The professional should assume that the woman

A.   is using denial as a defense mechanism
B.   has entered the first phase of the separation cycle
C.   has begun to rely on dissociation as a defense mechanism
D.   has acquired a personality disorder

25)   A certified copy of an order of protection generally contains a stamp, 25. _____
seal, or signature of the issuing judge or clerk of court, and a notation that the
copy is an authentic duplicate of the original order of the court. Which of the
following statements about certification is TRUE?

I.   The Violence Against Women Act mandates that an order of
        protection be certified in order to be enforceable across state,
        territorial, or tribal lines
II.   Many jurisdictions require that a copy of a foreign order be
        certified for purposes of registration or filing.
III.   A copy of an order of protection is generally not considered
        valid by any applicable authority unless certified.

A.   I only
B.   I and II
C.   II only
D.   I, II and III

KEY (CORRECT ANSWERS)

1. C
2. D
3. B
4. C
5. B

6. C
7. D
8. B
9. B
10. A

11. B
12. A
13. A
14. A
15. A

16. D
17. D
18. C
19. A
20. D

21. A
22. D
23. A
24. C
25. C

TEST 3

Directions: Each question or incomplete statement is followed by several suggested answers or completions. Select the one the BEST answers the question or completes the statement. *PRINT THE LETTER OF THE CORRECT ANSWER IN THE SPACE AT THE RIGHT.*

1)   When stalking takes place in conjunction with domestic violence, it is MOST likely to be associated with the

1. _____

A.   the tension-building phase
B.   the battering episode
C.   the reconciliation period
D.   battered spouse's decision to end the cycle of violence

2)   The "cycle of violence" with respect to domestic violence means that:

2. _____

A.   children who witness domestic violence between their parents do not grow up to become batterers themselves
B.   spousal violence grows over the years until one partner finally kills the other
C.   a battery takes place after a tension-building phase and is followed by a period of reconciliation
D.   eventually the woman will leave or divorce the husband

3)   The withholding of basic food, clothing and shelter from an aged victim by a caretaker is characterized as:

3. _____

A.   abuse
B.   neglect
C.   aggravated elderly abuse
D.   third degree assault

4)   Batterers generally

4. _____

        I.   deny responsibility for their actions
        II.   take a long time to commit to a monogamous relationship
        III.   have an excessive need for control
        IV.   try to cut partners off from outside resources

A.   I and II
B.   I, III and IV
C.   III and IV
D.   I, II, III and IV

5) A woman visits a domestic violence shelter and wants to talk with a   5. _____
worker there. The woman thinks she might be being abused by her boyfriend,
but she is confused about what constitutes "abuse." Questions the worker
might ask include

I.   After he has hit you, does he act sweet and loving?
II. Has he forced you to have sex?
III. What kind of situations precipitate his violent behavior?
IV. Has he caused you to be late or to miss work?

A. I and II
B. I, II and IV
C. II only
D. I, II, III and IV

6) Under the full faith and credit provisions of the Violence Against   6. _____
Women Act, a consent order

A. does not require a finding of abuse in order to be enforceable
B. is enforceable against the respondent, but not the petitioner, unless
there has been a cross-filing
C. is a criminal order of protection
D. is not enforceable

7) Which of the following variables would most likely be classified as   7. _____
constituting no risk or a low risk for child abuse?

A. Family is geographically isolated from community services
B. A caretaker who is overly compliant with the investigator
C. An injury on the child's torso
D. One previous report of abuse

8) Which of the following is a major reason why domestic violence   8. _____
victims do not report abuse to the police?

A. Apathy
B. Language barriers
C. Uncertainty about whether a crime was committed
D. They don't think the police will do anything

9)   Studies of domestic violence victims have suggested that about   9. _____
_____ percent of those who are employed experience some type of
problem in the workplace as a direct result of the abuse or abuser.

A.   25
B.   45
C.   75
D.   95

10)   Indian tribes recognize protection orders from other jurisdictions under   10. _____
the legal principle of

A.   comity
B.   double jeopardy
C.   full faith and credit
D.   vicarious liability

11)   The phenomenon known as "secondary victimization" involves each   11. _____
of the following, EXCEPT

A.   the victim's family and friends
B.   the criminal justice system
C.   the offender
D.   victim compensation programs

12)   The sibling of a physically abused child has approximately a   12. _____
_____ percent chance of being abused at the same time.

A.   20
B.   40
C.   60
D.   80

13)   Mandates of the Victims of Child Abuse Act of 1990 include   13. _____

        I.   permitting testimony via two-way closed circuit television in
                certain circumstances
        II.   limiting the scope of competency examinations for children
                unless ordered by a judge
        III.   consultation with multi-disciplinary teams for information on
                professional evaluations
        IV.   accompaniment throughout the trial by an adult attendant

A.   I only
B.   I and IV
C.   II, III, and IV
D.   I, II, III and IV

14) A woman is not yet ready to leave her abusive husband, but is willing
to work with a domestic violence professional on a safety plan for minimizing
risks and injuries during a battering episode. One of the strategies in such a
plan is to identify safe areas of the house. Of the following, the safest area is
probably the

14. _____

A. bedroom
B. kitchen
C. bathroom
D. garage

15) Of the perpetrators of child maltreatment in the United States, approximately what percentage are parents?

15. _____

A. 25
B. 50
C. 75
D. 95

16) Which of the following offenses would typically NOT be classified as
a Family Offense Misdemeanor?

16. _____

A. An assault that breaks a bone
B. Harassment over the phone
C. An assault that causes substantial pain
D. An assault that impairs the victims' physical condition

17) Infants who are born prematurely are proportionally over-represented
in the population of physically abused infants and children. Each of the
following is a likely factor in this situation, EXCEPT

17. _____

A. long initial separation from parents
B. lower standard of "abuse" due to physical frailty
C. parental feelings of disappointment and guilt
D. infant difficulty in recognizing and responding to caregiving behaviors

18) It is estimated that approximately _____ percent of all battered
women who seek help have diagnosable post-traumatic stress disorder
(PTSD).

18. _____

A. 10
B. 30
C. 50
D. 75

19) Which of the following is NOT a physiological explanation for rape?   19. _____

A.   uncontrollable sex drive
B.   lack of available partners
C.   sublimation of repressed desires
D.   consequence of the natural selection process

20) Because many parents believe in and utilize corporal punishment as   20. _____
discipline, a professional must be able to differentiate physical abuse from
ordinary spanking or corporal punishment. Which of the following is NOT a
useful means of making this distinction?

A.   Parent striking the child in places that are easily injured
B.   Repeated episodes of corporal punishment
C.   Child's report that punishments are severe and painful
D.   Injury to child's body tissue

21) The decision to confirm a report of child abuse or neglect is likely to   21. _____
rely on each of the following, EXCEPT

A.   the intent of the perpetrator
B.   the availability of community resources that may help reduce the risk
of abuse or neglect
C.   the degree to which the worker is certain that an injury was caused by
willful or negligent acts of the caretaker or perpetrator
D.   information regarding past incidents or reports

22) According to the law in most states, a person arrested for domestic   22. _____
violence typically

A.   may be released on bail only if he or she promises not to return to the
scene of the offense and commit another act of violence
B.   is eligible for release on his or her own recognizance (ROR) prior to
first appearance before a judge or magistrate
C.   is not entitled to bail prior to first appearance
D.   has 30 days in which to vacate the domicile

23) Which of the following is a national child abuse prevention organiza-   23. _____
tion that relies on mutual support and parent leadership?

A.   Parents Anonymous
B.   The National Coalition Against Domestic Violence
C.   The Office of Juvenile Justice and Delinquency Prevention
D.   Childhelp USA

24) When leaving a violent domestic situation behind, a victim should generally do each of the following, EXCEPT

24. _____

A. provide relatives with relocation information
B. avoid the use of credit cards
C. take all important documents upon departure
D. ask the police to supervise as belongings are removed, and to escort the departure

25) A woman has left her abusive husband and wants to get her name legally changed, in order to make it more difficult for her abuser to find her. State laws for name changes usually require publication. The woman wants to limit access to the knowledge of her new name, while still having the name recognized by the Social Security Administration and other parties. Usually, the options available to the woman include

25. _____

   I. making a motion for her to notify each required party (creditors, agencies, the military) directly, without publication
   II. request publication of a notice that simply says she is changing her name, without saying what her new name will be, and indicating that anyone with questions can contact her lawyer.
   III. simply notifying each interested party (creditors, etc.) of the name change, without going through the courts
   IV. first applying for a new Social Security Number, under a different name, and then notify each interested party of the changes

A. I and II
B. II only
C. II and III
D. II, III and IV

KEY (CORRECT ANSWERS)

1. D
2. C
3. B
4. B
5. A

6. A
7. C
8. D
9. D
10. A

11. C
12. A
13. D
14. A
15. C

16. A
17. B
18. C
19. C
20. C

21. B
22. C
23. A
24. A
25. A

EXAMINATION SECTION
TEST 1

DIRECTIONS: Each question or incomplete statement is followed by several suggested answers or completions. Select the one that BEST answers the question or completes the statement. *PRINT THE LETTER OF THE CORRECT ANSWER IN THE SPACE AT THE RIGHT.*

Questions 1-13.

DIRECTIONS: Questions 1 through 13 are to be answered on the basis of the following information.

Sonny Burnett, a drug addict, is admitted to the hospital and is suspected of having hepatitis. The diagnosis of Type B hepatitis is confirmed, and Sonny is placed in a unit with other drug addicts. A decision to attempt a *cold turkey* withdrawal for Sonny is made by the health team.

1. Which of the following observations indicates that Sonny   1.___
   has recently had a *fix*?
   A. Increased blood pressure
   B. Fruity breath
   C. Needle marks on his extremities
   D. Constricted pupils

2. Which of the following statements should be included in   2.___
   the nurse's instructions to Sonny concerning his illness?
   A. Treatment with hepatitis B immune globulin will
      provide you with immunity.
   B. You have developed an immunity to viral hepatitis.
   C. You will have a lifelong immunity to serum hepatitis.
   D. You will always be more susceptible to serum hepatitis.

3. To prevent the spread of the disease to others, the nurse   3.___
   should place Sonny on _____ isolation precautions.
   A. blood and body fluids
   B. respiratory and body fluids
   C. respiratory and enteric
   D. enteric and blood

4. The nursing care plan includes expanding the range of   4.___
   interests of the clients in Sonny's group.
   The MOST therapeutic initial approach would be to
   A. accept the group's need to communicate in the addict's
      jargon
   B. speak to the group about the harmful effects of drug
      abuse
   C. support the group members in their need to discuss
      their habit
   D. discourage the group from discussing drugs or having
      gutter talk

5. The symptoms that Sonny would MOST likely exhibit at the   5.__
   onset of *cold turkey* withdrawal are
      A. weight loss, severe stomach cramps, and vomiting
      B. muscular pain, anorexia, and diarrhea
      C. diaphoresis, yawning, lacrimation, and sneezing
      D. restlessness, insomnia, and increased blood pressure

6. Sonny asks the nurse how long he is going to suffer the   6.__
   withdrawal symptoms.
   The MOST accurate reply by the nurse would be that if you
   just started withdrawal, symptoms should begin in _____
   hours, peak in _____, and subside in _____.
      A. 4; 24 hours; 48 hours   B. 12; 36 hours; 72 hours
      C. 24; 3 days; 5 days   D. 36; 5 days; 7 days

7. The MOST therapeutic action by the nurse during the peak   7.__
   phase of Sonny's withdrawal from heroin would be
      A. providing adequate fluid intake
      B. providing a supplementary diet
      C. instituting convulsion precautions
      D. administering prescribed sedation

8. Sonny's laboratory findings show a slight improvement, but   8.__
   he is suffering from appetite loss.
   To ensure adequate nutrition, the nurse should
      A. request an order for intravenous fluid and vitamin
         therapy
      B. weigh Sonny at least every second day and keep him
         informed of his weight changes
      C. provide Sonny with small meals and high-protein
         beverages between meals
      D. encourage ambulation to stimulate Sonny's appetite

9. Sonny was found with the following symptoms during his   9.__
   withdrawal from heroin.
   Which set of symptoms suggests a complication that would
   require IMMEDIATE nursing intervention?
      A. Marked rise in temperature or blood pressure, or both
      B. Anxiety, tremors, and depression
      C. Nausea, vomiting, and diarrhea
      D. Profuse diaphoresis, influenza symptoms, and chills

10. Sonny and the health care team discuss what type of   10.__
    environment he needs for best recovery from his drug
    problem and decide on a structured environment.
    Of the following characteristics of this environment,
    the one that will be of GREATEST basic benefit to Sonny is
       A. having others tell him what to do
       B. knowing what the rules are and what is expected of him
       C. being protected from outside influences
       D. learning more about the effects of drugs

11. Sonny, after noticing and being curious, asks the nurse   11.___
    why some of the clients are receiving methadone as a
    replacement for heroin.
    The BEST reply by the nurse would be that this narcotic
    is given because it
       A. cannot be taken with other drugs
       B. is nonaddictive
       C. gives a euphoric feeling
       D. relieves withdrawal symptoms

12. Sonny asks the nurse why it is necessary for one to have a   12.___
    periodic urine test when taking methadone.
    Which of the following would be the BEST reply by the
    nurse?
       A. We need to test the kidneys' threshold to methadone.
       B. Methadone irritates the kidneys, so we have to do a
          kidney function test.
       C. We test for drugs other than methadone.
       D. We have to determine the methadone dosage.

13. Sonny wants to know why heroin causes hepatitis.   13.___
    The explanation by the nurse that would be MOST appropriate
    for Sonny is:
       A. Heroin reduces one's natural defenses
       B. Hepatitis is not caused by heroin
       C. Hepatitis is caused by a germ found on the skin
       D. Hepatitis is caused by using dirty needles

Questions 14-18.

DIRECTIONS: Questions 14 through 18 are to be answered on the
              basis of the following information.

    Linda Carter, age 24, just got discharged from the hospital
after being treated for substance abuse. She is addicted to alcohol
and cocaine. She is now seeing Ms. Flores, the nurse at the local
mental health center.

14. Ms. Flores plans to help Linda adjust to the activities   14.___
    of the community mental health center.
    The FIRST action taken by the nurse should be to
       A. ask for a detailed history of threatened drug abuse
       B. assess her own feelings about the client's lack of
          control
       C. assign the client to a volunteer who also has had a
          drug problem
       D. introduce herself and state her objectives

15. Linda tells the group at the health center that her   15.___
    drinking was caused by her family, who all drank like fish.
    How should the nurse analyze this behavior?
       A. Linda's family was the cause of her drug use.
       B. Most users get addicted to drugs through their families.

C. The behavior of most drug users is aggression turned outward.
D. Linda does not take responsibility for her drug use.

16. Linda comes to the center with alcohol odor on her breath. 16.___
    The nurse should
    A. assign her to an Alcoholics Anonymous group meeting
    B. call her family to come and take her home
    C. ask her what happened to make her want a drink
    D. tell her that she cannot come to the center while drinking

17. Linda tells the nurse that she always felt she wasn't 17.___
    good enough, and with drugs she felt she was the greatest.
    The BEST plan of action for her at this time would be to
    A. suggest that she put trust in a supreme being
    B. offer recognition for accomplishing tasks
    C. encourage her to talk to others who have similar problems
    D. recommend that she live life one day at a time

18. Another important plan for the future that Linda and 18.___
    the nurse should make to help her overcome her addictive
    behavior is that she must
    A. not resume a relationship with her old drinking friends
    B. find a time-filling and gratifying occupation
    C. not attend any social gatherings without a chaperone
    D. move back into the protective environment of her family

Questions 19-28.

DIRECTIONS: Questions 19 through 28 are to be answered on the basis of the following information.

Burt Right, 28 years old, has a history of juvenile offenses, having an arrogant manner, always being a loner, and preferring to do things his own way. He can see no wrong in himself and no right in others.

Due to his aggressive behavior, he once got involved in a serious fight and got shot in the right leg. While Burt's physical condition has been improving, he continually demonstrates disruptive behavior. He has been arrogant and demanding.

19. After a psychiatric consultation, Burt is diagnosed as 19.___
    having antisocial behavior.
    Which problem exhibited by the client would be the MOST
    difficult for the staff to handle?
    A. Having problems in distinguishing true statements from lies
    B. Not being able to form a close relationship
    C. Being persistent in his antisocial behavior
    D. Not learning from experience

20. Burt is transferred to a psychiatric unit. During orien-
    tation, Burt is told of the rules and regulations of the
    unit. One day, he borrows another person's shampoo with-
    out permission. He says to the nurse, *It's not stealing
    when you borrow shampoo*.
    The nurse's BEST response in this situation is:
    A. Keep the shampoo; I will get more for the other
       patient.
    B. Give the client his shampoo back and tell him you
       are sorry
    C. You will not be penalized; the rules do not include
       borrowing shampoo
    D. The rule is, when you steal you will be penalized

    20.____

21. When Burt is confronted about his unacceptable behavior
    toward others, the staff should expect him to
    A. become very angry
    B. accept the criticism
    C. show very little concern
    D. withdraw from others

    21.____

22. The group which would probably provide the MOST therapeutic
    advice in the course of determining penalties for breaking
    the rules of the mental health unit would be the
    A. clients who live in the unit and have to abide by the
       rules
    B. lay people in the community who determine hospital
       policy
    C. members of the administrative group who determine
       the rules of the hospital
    D. members of the mental health professional staff who
       set the standards of the unit

    22.____

23. Which approach by the nursing team would be MOST effective
    with Burt?
    A. Providing a nonstructured environment
    B. Being a part of the therapeutic community
    C. A one-to-one relationship
    D. Allowing Burt to direct his treatment

    23.____

24. Burt appears to be very reliable, has excellent reasoning,
    is not reacting in an emotionally disturbed way, and his
    actions seem to be completely normal.
    The nurse can BEST assess his behavior through obtaining
    A. Burt's cooperation and consent
    B. a series of psychological tests
    C. a detailed history from Burt
    D. his behavioral history from acquaintances

    24.____

25. The health team has been observing Burt's interactions
    with members of his family.
    Which behavior of the family would MOST likely contribute
    to Burt's illness?

    25.____

A. Being overprotective, hypochondriacal, symbiotic, and dependent
B. Violence, indifference, rejection, and lack of predictability
C. Using sexual provocation and being compulsive and rigid
D. Setting goals too high, and thus making Burt feel guilty

26. The members of the staff have started having difficulty   26.___
accepting Burt and have started criticizing him even when
he has not broken a rule.
The PROBABLE reason for this nontherapeutic approach is
that
    A. Burt's behavior is very destructive to others
    B. Burt's behavior is considered pathological
    C. Burt does not reinforce the staff for its efforts
    D. the staff can show Burt that inconsistency is not
       therapeutic

27. The nurse analyzing Burt's behavior recognizes that he is   27.___
often in conflict with others because he has
    A. disguised his deep feelings for others
    B. never learned group norms and loyalty
    C. reverted to regressive patterns of behavior
    D. lived his life in an asocial environment

28. Burt and his family have been in therapy for eight months.   28.___
Burt is receiving therapy through the hospital clinic.
In evaluating Burt's progress, the health team is most
likely to observe that Burt shows internalized acceptable
behavior MOST often
    A. when interacting with the clients
    B. after talking to the nursing staff
    C. after visits with his family
    D. during the hourly sessions with his doctor

Questions 29-30.

DIRECTIONS: Questions 29 and 30 are to be answered on the basis
              of the following information.

    A client of yours is Jill Lebensfield, who is 30 years old.
She was admitted because she had attacked her neighbor with a knife
as, according to her, the neighbor was unlawfully wiretapping her
house. She continues to feel that others are spying on her.

29. Jill tells the nurse, *I'm not crazy; I don't belong here,*   29.___
    my neighbor does.
    What behavior pattern is she using?
        A. Sociopathic   B. Aggressive
        C. Neurotic   D. Projective

30. Jill uses this behavior because   30.___
    A. she never learned to control her temper
    B. it is a secondary gain of aggressive behavior
    C. some aspects of her life are difficult to handle
    D. social-moral codes were never learned

———

KEY (CORRECT ANSWERS)

1. D		11. D		21. C	
2. C		12. C		22. A	
3. A		13. D		23. B	
4. D		14. B		24. D	
5. C		15. D		25. B	
6. B		16. C		26. C	
7. A		17. B		27. B	
8. C		18. A		28. A	
9. A		19. D		29. D	
10. B		20. D		30. C	

———

TEST 2

DIRECTIONS: Each question or incomplete statement is followed by several suggested answers or completions. Select the one that BEST answers the question or completes the statement. *PRINT THE LETTER OF THE CORRECT ANSWER IN THE SPACE AT THE RIGHT.*

Questions 1-11.

DIRECTIONS: Questions 1 through 11 are to be answered on the basis of the following information.

Norman Bates, 24 years old, is brought to the emergency mental health center by his family. He had furiously tried to attack his mother. For the last 6 months, since graduating from college, he has not been able to find employment, and most of the time he sits and stares into space. On admission, he appears dazed and speaks incoherently.

1. The nurse observes that Mr. Bates sits alone in the dayroom staring at the floor. His clothes are disheveled, and his hair and beard are unkempt. She approaches him and intro-duces herself as his primary nurse.
   Which statement would be MOST appropriate by the nurse at this time?
   A. There is a meeting of all new clients and I will introduce you.
   B. I will sit with you for 10 minutes. You don't have to talk.
   C. This is the hour for occupational therapy. I will go with you.
   D. If you care to, you may go to your room. You had a difficult night.

1.___

2. The nurse observes Mr. Bates sitting alone. He is staring into space, smiling, and moving his lips as if talking to someone.
   How should the nurse approach him?
   A. What do you see when you stare into space?
   B. You must not sit by yourself; you will hear voices.
   C. Tell me what the voices are telling you.
   D. You were moving your lips, but made no sound.

2.___

3. Mr. Bates tells the nurse that he hears voices telling him he is a good person.
   The MOST accurate reply by the nurse would be:
   A. A stimulating environment can enhance one's senses and cause hallucinations.
   B. You have an overactive imagination that makes up for a dull existence.

3.___

C. There are unconscious feelings breaking into your
   consciousness.
D. There must be some pathology to the sensory organ
   receptors or nerves.

4. Mr. Bates asks the nurse when the best time to try to
   control the voices would be.
   Which reply would be MOST accurate?
   _____ the voices.
   A. When you are actively hearing
   B. When you are not hearing
   C. When you are waiting to hear
   D. Immediately after hearing

4.____

5. Mr. Bates tells the nurse, *You have a time to contact the
   individual.* The nurse recognizes that this is speech that
   has meaning only for the client in his primitive thoughts.
   What type of speech is this?
   A. Word salad   B. Magical thinking
   C. Looseness of association D. Neologisms

5.____

6. Mr. Bates asks the nurse to give him an example of his
   behavior that the doctor called *delusions of reference.*
   Which reply by the nurse would be ACCURATE?
   A. The room is wired by the police, who want to get me.
   B. My body is disintegrating into a mass of jelly.
   C. I'm the prince of Wales; my name is Charles.
   D. The conversations and actions of others are always
      concerning me.

6.____

7. The nurse tells Mr. Bates that the long-term goal for the
   nurse/client therapeutic sessions is to help him
   A. accept his behavior and not feel guilty
   B. learn to communicate in a less symbolic way
   C. understand the reason for his sick behavior
   D. learn new skills so that he can find employment

7.____

8. After several weeks of daily therapeutic sessions, Mr.
   Bates tells the nurse, *You are like everyone else; you
   don't understand me - you are pushing.*
   How should the nurse reply?
   A. Do you feel that I have been pushing you too fast?
   B. Not being understood must be very difficult.
   C. Who is this everyone else I remind you of?
   D. Maybe we should find someone else to replace me.

8.____

9. Mr. Bates asks the nurse why so many clients return to
   the hospital after being discharged.
   The MAIN reason for this revolving-door syndrome is
   A. families and the community reject the client
   B. the client refuses to return for follow-up care in
      the community
   C. the client cannot find suitable employment
   D. a symbiotic relationship has developed with the staff

9.____

10. The nurse and Mr. Bates are ready to plan for his partici-   10.__
    pation in groups.
    Before making this plan, it should be considered whether
    he
    A. is accepted by other clients on the unit
    B. is ready to be discharged from the hospital
    C. can tolerate the nurse without stress
    D. still needs the nurse's support

11. A week before his discharge, Mr. Bates and the nurse go   11.__
    on a shopping trip.
    The MAIN objective of this activity is to
    A. boost Mr. Bates' self-esteem by providing diversional
       activity in the community
    B. give Mr. Bates an opportunity to buy some clothes
    C. assist Mr. Bates in implementing some skills he
       learned in the hospital
    D. condition Mr. Bates toward acceptable behavior in
       the community

Questions 12-30.

DIRECTIONS: Questions 12 through 30 are to be answered on the
              basis of the following information.

     Bobby Briggs, age 20, has been hospitalized for 14 days with
compound fractures of the right tibia and fibula resulting from a
motorcycle accident. After closed reduction of the fractures, he
is placed in traction. His personality evaluation indicates that
he is a shy, introspective person who keeps to himself and never
talks unless asked a direct question. He has had no visitors.

12. Bobby's nurse assesses his emotional problem.   12.__
    The nurse understands that, at his age, a PRIMARY develop-
    mental task is to
    A. have a sense of self and extended self in an intimate
       relationship
    B. seek to become a part of a group with a sense of
       belonging to this group
    C. have identified life's goals such as occupational
       and marital choices
    D. gain feelings of self-worth as a result of appraisals
       from significant others

13. The nurse observes that Bobby appears very insecure.   13.__
    The MOST effective nursing action in helping to alleviate
    Bobby's insecurity would be to
    A. allow him freedom to do what he wants
    B. plan a consistent staff approach based on his needs
    C. provide for his physical and emotional needs
    D. assign someone to be with him until his anxiety
       subsides

14. The nurse understands that Bobby's withdrawn behavior is   14.___
MOST likely due to the fact that
   A. there is a constant need for approval, yet he resents
      it
   B. he has identified with the parent who lacks superego
      control
   C. he has received too much protection from significant
      others
   D. interpersonal relationships become a source of anxiety

15. The nurse also understands that Bobby's behavior is a   15.___
defense, because the world of reality is painful for him.
Which behavior should the nurse observe to confirm this?
   A. He avoids relationships by staying at a safe and
      familiar level of functioning.
   B. His emotions have created visceral changes and he has
      repressed his emotions.
   C. He can admit no fault in himself or any virtue in
      others.
   D. He is preoccupied with a sense of self-depreciation
      and self-reproach.

16. The nurse has planned a series of interviews with Bobby.   16.___
The nurse should place the chair _____ from the client,
to provide an appropriate space.
   A. 4 to 8 inches   B. 8 to 24 inches
   C. 18 inches to 4 feet   D. 4 to 8 feet

17. The nurse understands that at this distance the nurse   17.___
and client are more comfortable because
   A. the voice can be kept at a whisper
   B. fine details of the other person are lost
   C. they can touch one another without reaching
   D. vision and perception are not distorted

18. The nurse makes an appointment with Bobby to talk to him   18.___
daily for approximately 30 minutes.
The nurse's PRIMARY goal in arranging these meetings is to
   A. aid Bobby with his socializing problem by socializing
      with him
   B. assist in identifying his problems in a one-to-one
      relationship
   C. help have a feeling that others in the environment
      care
   D. determine from Bobby why he is so withdrawn and has
      no friends

19. After being introduced, Bobby does not acknowledge the   19.___
nurse's presence.
The nurse should know that
   A. admission to a new environment causes him to withdraw
   B. he needs rest if proper healing is to take place
   C. the accident may also have caused some brain injury
   D. rejection of interpersonal relationships is part of
      his defense

20. The FIRST short-term goal for the nurse to establish as a nursing care need of Bobby should be to
    A. establish and maintain the client's contact with reality
    B. provide for trust and security in the nurse/client relationship
    C. initiate and develop the nurse/client relationship
    D. encourage and support the client's interactions with others

20.__

21. At an early session, Bobby complains of discomfort in his lower back.
    What action by the nurse would BEST meet Bobby's needs?
    A. Give him simple instructions for isometric exercises for the back.
    B. Give him his prn medication of Tylenol, 1000 mg.
    C. Give him a back rub while he raises his hip.
    D. Ask him when he had his last bowel movement.

21.__

22. The nurse implements nursing care to alleviate Bobby's back pain because
    A. physical touching will alleviate pain and also provide trust and security needed
    B. lack of bowel movement can cause pressure on the lower back
    C. isometric exercises will strengthen muscles and prevent atrophy
    D. Tylenol reduces pain caused by muscle spasms

22.__

23. Bobby tells the nurse that he has always liked to be alone. He states, *You know, the best company is my own*.
    Which reply by the nurse would BEST expand his experience?
    A. You have a great deal of self-confidence, don't you?
    B. Are you saying you never enjoy the company of others?
    C. Tell me how it makes you feel to be with others.
    D. You will miss a lot of life by being a loner.

23.__

24. Although Bobby answers direct questions, there are long periods of silence.
    The nurse understands that Bobby is using this silence because he is
    A. thinking of what to say
    B. clarifying his thoughts
    C. severely depressed
    D. uncomfortable with others

24.__

25. The nurse can BEST break the silence with Bobby by saying:
    A. If I'm upsetting you, I'll be back later
    B. It must be difficult to talk to strangers
    C. What are you thinking about?
    D. Do these sessions with me make you nervous?

25.__

26. The nurse observes that Bobby cracks his knuckles whenever   26.___
    he is anxious.
    Which nursing action would be MOST therapeutic?
       A. Give him something to do with his hands so he will be
          occupied.
       B. Ask the physician to prescribe a mild tranquilizer
          for him.
       C. Explain to Bobby that this behavior will make his
          hands arthritic.
       D. Assess what causes this behavior and take steps to
          lessen his discomfort.

27. At another session, Bobby tells the nurse that his brother   27.___
    was to blame for the motorcycle accident. He states that
    if his brother hadn't sold it to him, he wouldn't be in
    this fix today.
    The nurse understands that this statement reflects
       A. avoidance of a close relationship with his brother
       B. an impression that a different cycle would have been
          safer
       C. dislike of his brother who sold a defective cycle
       D. feelings of failure that he attributes to his brother

28. After Bobby made the statement blaming his brother for the   28.___
    accident, the nurse should reply:
       A. What do you and your family do for pleasure when you
          are together?
       B. This must be a difficult time for you. How did the
          accident happen?
       C. You feel that your brother sold you an inferior bike.
       D. It must be difficult for you being in pain, while
          your brother is not.

29. Bobby's health condition has improved.   29.___
    The observation by the nurse that indicates that Bobby's
    emotional health has also improved is that he
       A. is able to talk about his problem and not withdraw
       B. gives the staff a box of chocolate for helping him
       C. tells the nurse he can work on his problems alone
       D. discontinues the sessions with the nurse therapist

30. Which referral group would be MOST beneficial for Bobby   30.___
    at the time he leaves the hospital?
       A. Group of people who have problems communicating
       B. Safety driving school for motorcyclists
       C. Public health department for follow-up care
       D. Encounter group where Bobby will be forced to look
          at his behavior

KEY (CORRECT ANSWERS)

1. D	11. D	21. C
2. B	12. A	22. A
3. C	13. B	23. C
4. C	14. D	24. D
5. A	15. A	25. B
6. D	16. C	26. D
7. B	17. D	27. D
8. C	18. B	28. B
9. B	19. D	29. A
10. C	20. C	30. C

EXAMINATION SECTION
TEST 1

DIRECTIONS: Each question or incomplete statement is followed by
several suggested answers or completions. Select the
one that BEST answers the question or completes the
statement. *PRINT THE LETTER OF THE CORRECT ANSWER IN
THE SPACE AT THE RIGHT.*

1. Which amendments to the Constitution limit the power of   1.___
   the federal government to discriminate in employment?
   A. 2nd and 12th   B. 3rd and 8th
   C. 4th and 9th   D. 5th and 14th

2. In sexual harassment investigations involving co-workers,   2.___
   the investigator should look most closely at the
   A. presumption of knowledge on the part of the co-worker
   B. nature of the behavior
   C. overall effect of the co-worker's behavior on the
      workplace atmosphere
   D. relative power of the co-worker compared to the
      plaintiff

3. Which of the following causes of action may be indicated   3.___
   if an HIV-infected individual knowingly exposes another
   person to the disease without forewarning?
     I. Negligence
    II. Battery
   III. Intentional Infliction of Emotional Distress
    IV. Fraud

   The CORRECT answer is:
   A. I, II   B. II, III   C. III, IV   D. I, IV

4. Which of the following is NOT a federal requirement   4.___
   involving child labor?
   A. Children attending school and at least 14 years old
      are permitted to work outside of school hours
      provided they work no more than 3 hours on a school
      day.
   B. Under no conditions may a student in grades up to 12
      work in jobs declared hazardous by the Secretary of
      Labor.
   C. Children attending school and at least 14 years old
      are prohibited from working more than 8 hours on a
      non-school day.
   D. Work may not begin before 7 A.M. or end after 7 P.M.
      during the school year.

5. Which of the following federal laws established the Equal   5.___
   Employment Opportunity Commission (EEOC)?
   The
   A. Fair Labor Standards Act of 1938
   B. Landrum-Griffin Act of 1959
   C. Civil Rights Act of 1964
   D. Age Discrimination in Employment Act of 1967

6. The *new construction* requirements of the Americans with
    Disabilities Act (ADA) of 1990 apply to buildings which
    were first occupied after
    A. March 11, 1990   B. August 11, 1991
    C. January 26, 1993   D. November 4, 1995

6._

7. Workers who believe they have been terminated as a result
    of a *whistleblower* who reported unsafe workplace conditions
    can generally file a complaint with OSHA within _____ of
    the alleged incident.
    A. 30 days   B. 90 days   C. 180 days   D. 1 year

7._

8. In general, a landlord is entitled to reject a rental
    application for each of the following reasons EXCEPT
    A. insufficient income
    B. past negative behavior such as property damage
    C. marital status or cohabitation that conflicts with
       the landlord's moral principles
    D. bad credit history

8._

9. Under the terms of the Employee Retirement Income Security
    Act (ERISA) of 1974, employers have several options for
    granting vesting rights to employees. Which of the
    following is not one of these?
    A. Ten-year vesting
    B. Five-year vesting
    C. Graded vesting
    D. 50% vesting when the total of an employee's age and
       length of employment equals 45 years

9._

10. Regardless of whether the EEOC has completed its own
    investigation, an employee who wants to bring a private
    civil suit against an employer is entitled to do so __ days
    after filing the complaint.
    A. 30   B. 60   C. 180   D. 300

10._

11. To which of the following actions, performed by an owner,
    landlord, or tenant seeking a roommate, do the discrimina-
    tion provisions of the Federal Fair Housing Act apply?
      I. Refuse to negotiate for housing
     II. Set different terms, conditions or privileges for
         sale or rental of a dwelling
    III. Persuade owners to sell or rent
     IV. Provide different housing services or facilities

    The CORRECT answer is:
    A. I, III   B. II, IV
    C. II, III   D. I, II, III, IV

11._

12. Each of the following is an eligibility requirement for
    an employee seeking benefits under the Family Medical Leave
    Act (FMLA) of 1993 EXCEPT that he or she must
    A. have worked for the covered employer for a total of
       at least 12 months
    B. not be classified as an agricultural worker

12._

   C. have worked for a minimum of 1,250 hours in the
      previous 12 months
   D. work at a location within the United States or its
      territories or possessions

13. Which of the following types of immigrants is NOT pro-   13.___
    tected by the discrimination provisions of federal
    immigration legislation?
       A. Refugees   B. Permanent residents
       C. Asylees   D. Undocumented residents

14. The Equal Access Act of 1984, which was intended to   14.___
    protect religious speech in an educational environment,
    applies to _____ receiving federal funds.
       A. all K-12 public schools
       B. all colleges and universities
       C. public secondary schools
       D. public or private secondary schools

15. Once a job offer has been made, an employer may condition   15.___
    employment upon a satisfactory medical examination if it
    can be demonstrated that
       A. all applicants have to submit to the same examination
       B. the results of the examination will be kept confiden-
          tial
       C. the examination does not specifically test for
          disability
       D. the results of the examination had no relevance to
          the hiring decision

16. Under the provisions of the Americans with Disabilities   16.___
    Act (ADA) of 1990, van-accessible parking spaces for
    disabled individuals must have an access aisle that is
    at least _____ feet wide.
       A. 4   B. 6   C. 8   D. 10

17. To which of the following types of organizations would   17.___
    federal AIDS discrimination legislation apply?
       I. A bona fide private membership club
      II. Corporations wholly owned by the United States
     III. Employment agencies
      IV. Corporations wholly owned by an Indian tribe

    The CORRECT answer is:
       A. II, III   B. III *only*   C. IV *only*   D. I, II

18. Federal minimum wage legislation requires that overtime   18.___
    work be compensated at a rate that is at least _____%
    of the rate of pay for normal working hours.
       A. 100   B. 125   C. 150   D. 200

19. In terms of human rights, *deferral states* are those that   19.___
       A. rely on the EEOC for investigation into claims of
          discrimination
       B. have shorter time limits on filing claims

     C. send claims directly to a federal district court
     D. make their own investigations prior to those of the
        EEOC

20. Which of the following federal laws awarded attorney's
    fees and costs to parents who were successful in litiga-
    tion?
    The
     A. Rehabilitation Act of 1973
     B. Education for All Handicapped Children Act of 1975
     C. Handicapped Children's Protection Act (HCPA) of 1986
     D. Individuals with Disabilities Education Act (IDEA)
       of 1997

                                                  20.

21. In AIDS litigation, which of the following is most likely
    to be the context for a cause of action for negligence?
     A. A tainted blood transfusion
     B. A sexual relationship
     C. The physician/patient relationship
     D. Exclusion from certain educational activities

                                                  21.

22. In 1980, the EEOC determined that
     A. gay, lesbian, or bisexual persons would be granted
       the same protections from discrimination as those
       of other groups
     B. sexual harassment is a form of gender discrimination
       that is prohibited under federal law
     C. privately-owned organizations are not subject to the
       same employment regulations as other groups
     D. persons with physical disabilities would be granted
       the same protections from discrimination as those of
       other groups

                                                  22.

23. Which of the following would be protected from hiring
    discrimination by the Americans with Disabilities Act
    (ADA) -- provided that he or she is qualified to perform
    the essential functions of the job?
    A(n)
      I. alcoholic
     II. person with AIDS
   III. person addicted to illegal drugs who is currently
       using
    IV. person with Down's Syndrome

    The CORRECT answer is:
     A. II *only*   B. II, IV
     C. I, II, IV   D. IV *only*

                                                  23.

24. In general, the maximum civil penalty for employers who
    violate OSHA provisions is
     A. $10,000   B. $70,000   C. $250,000   D. $500,000

                                                  24.

25. The Supreme Court's 1974 ruling in the case *Lemon v.*   25.___
Kurtzman established a precedent for how public schools
were expected to deal with the issue of
   A. attention deficit disorder (ADD)
   B. safety
   C. religious activity
   D. desegregation

KEY (CORRECT ANSWERS)

1. D	11. D
2. B	12. B
3. C	13. D
4. B	14. C
5. C	15. A
6. C	16. C
7. A	17. B
8. C	18. C
9. B	19. D
10. B	20. C

21. A
22. B
23. C
24. B
25. C

TEST 2

1. Under the provisions of the Family Medical Leave Act (FMLA) of 1993, which of the following are considered to be members of an employee's immediate family?
   I. Spouse   II. Children under 18
   III. Stepchildren under 18   IV. Parents

   The CORRECT answer is:
   A. I, II   B. I, II, III
   C. I, II, IV   D. II, IV

   1._

2. Which of the following groups are generally covered by federal equal employment opportunity laws?
   A. Indian tribes
   B. Agricultural workers
   C. Aliens employed by United States employers in foreign countries
   D. Publicly elected officials and members of their personal staff

   2._

3. In order to prevail in an age discrimination lawsuit, an employee has the burden of proving a prima facie case, which includes a demonstration of each of the following EXCEPT
   A. the employee is a member of the protected class, i.e., over the stipulated age
   B. the employee was adversely affected by the employer's action
   C. age was a determining factor in the employer's action
   D. the employer's action was willful

   3._

4. In determining whether disparate impact in a workplace is illegal, the EEOC's standard is that the rate of selection for minority applicants must be _____ the rate for whites.
   A. at least half   B. just over half
   C. at least four-fifths   D. equal to

   4._

5. Most likely to be covered by the provisions of the Occupational Safety and Health Act (OSHA) is a
   A. self-employed person   B. transportation worker
   C. textile worker   D. miner

   5._

6. Of the following, _____ is a permissible means by which an employer may attempt to influence the decisions of employees.
   A. closing down a plant permanently after an election to unionize

   6._

B. conferring economic benefits on employees prior to an election
C. locking out employees in order to prevent them from working
D. coercively interrogating employees about union activities

7. Which of the following are guaranteed protection from mandatory retirement under the provisions of the Age Discrimination in Employment Act?   7.___
   A. Air traffic controllers
   B. Tenured university faculty
   C. Senior middle managers at a private employer of more than 20 people
   D. Employees whose retirement pensions are worth $44,000 or more

8. Which of the following types of employers is most likely to be exempt from the provisions of the Fair Labor Standards Act?   8.___
   A. Local government agencies
   B. Employers who engage in interstate commerce
   C. Skilled laborers who employ apprentices
   D. Employers with annual sales of $500,000 or more

9. Which of the following types of rental units is most likely to be excepted from some of the federal statutes on housing discrimination?   9.___
   A
   A. detached unit that is on the same parcel of real property as the residence of the landlord
   B. single room in an owner-occupied home that does not house other lodgers
   C. multi-room, single-family home in a residential area in which most homes are inhabited by the owners
   D. single unit in an apartment complex

10. The *Opportunity Wage Provision* of federal wage law applies to employees who are   10.___
    A. under 18 years of age during their first 90 days of employment
    B. under 20 years of age during their first 90 days of employment
    C. under 18 years of age at any time during their employment
    D. legal immigrants

11. Under the provisions of federal law, which of the following are legitimate practices for a creditor to undertake in dealing with an elderly client?   11.___
    I. Closing a credit account based on the client's advanced age
    II. Using age as one of its factors in a credit scoring system

III. Considering whether a client's level of income will
continue for a particular duration
IV. Denying credit due to an applicant's advanced age
due to the default risk

The CORRECT answer is:
A. I, IV
B. II, III
C. I, II, III
D. I, II, IV

12. Each of the following is a factor involved in establish-   12.__
ing the *severe and pervasive* standard used in sexual
harassment investigations EXCEPT
   A. whether the behavior was directed at one or more
   individuals
   B. the position of the offender
   C. whether the behavior was welcome or not
   D. the type of behavior (physical/verbal)

13. Under the provisions of the Family Medical Leave Act   13.__
(FMLA) of 1993, a *key employee* is one who is
   A. directly or indirectly involved in at least 25 percent
   of all company revenues
   B. among the highest-paid ten percent of employees
   within 75 miles of the workplace
   C. the administrative head of any division which com-
   prises 10 percent or more of the total number of
   employees
   D. among the highest-paid ten percent of employees in a
   management position

14. Which of the following types of employers is most likely   14.__
to be subject to the provisions of the Employee Polygraph
Protection Act?
   A. Private providers of security services
   B. Private manufacturers of pharmaceuticals
   C. Private software manufacturers
   D. Federal government agencies

15. Which of the following constitutes *sponsorship* of   15.__
religious activity in schools?
   I. Assignment of a teacher to a religious meeting for
   custodial purposes
  II. Expending public funds for the incidental costs of
   providing space for student-initiated meetings
 III. Payment to a teacher for monitoring a student
   religious club
  IV. Using school media to announce meetings of student
   religious groups

The CORRECT answer is:
A. II, III
B. IV *only*
C. I *only*
D. None of the above

16. Federal labor laws permit an employer from barring an
    employee from soliciting other workers to engage in union
    activity when the
    A. employer can prove that the formation of a union
       will cause undue hardship
    B. employee is actually engaged in paid work
    C. employee is on company property
    D. employee is in areas that are open to the public

16.___

17. Rules on drug testing in schools
    A. are prohibited from being applied in public schools
    B. are entirely up to the school administration
    C. must follow certain federal guidelines
    D. are governed by guidelines that differ from state
       to state

17.___

18. Approximately what sector of the United States population
    is victimized by about 1/3 of all consumer fraud?
    A. Minors (under the age of 18)
    B. The elderly
    C. Young married couples
    D. Non-English speakers

18.___

19. Which of the following types of prayer is/are permitted
    in public schools?
      I. Voluntary participation in classroom prayer
     II. Moments of silent meditation for a classroom
    III. Student-led graduation prayers
     IV. Individual students praying quietly and unobtrusively

    The CORRECT answer is:
    A. I, II, IV   B. II, III
    C. IV *only*   D. I, III

19.___

20. Under the Americans with Disabilities Act (ADA) of 1990,
    privately-owned buildings are entitled to an *elevator
    exemption* if they are under three stories or
    A. are located on a grade of at least 10%
    B. are not devoted entirely to private residence
    C. consist of floors that are each under 3,000 square
       feet
    D. have been constructed after 1995

20.___

21. Title _____ of the Civil Rights Act of 1964 prohibits
    discrimination in federally-financed programs.
    A. II   B. IV   C. VI   D. IX

21.___

22. Each of the following is a federal law which affects AIDS
    and one's right to an education EXCEPT the
    A. Civil Rights Act of 1964
    B. Rehabilitation Act of 1974
    C. Americans with Disabilities Act of 1990
    D. Individuals with Disabilities Act (IDEA) of 1997

22.___

23. In the 1995 case *Vernonia v. Acton*, the Supreme Court ruled that a certain segment of the student population would be subject to drug and alcohol testing no matter what the circumstance. Which group was specified in this ruling?
    A. Student athletes
    B. Students with a known history of substance abuse
    C. Students whose parents requested testing
    D. Students in leadership or government positions

24. Under certain conditions, some types of properties may be exempt from federal fair housing law. Which of the following is NOT one of these?
    A. All owner-occupied buildings
    B. Property occupied solely by persons who are 62 or older
    C. Property owned by religious organizations
    D. Property owned by private clubs

25. Which of the following is TRUE of an economic strike?
    A. Employees remain eligible to vote.
    B. Employees must be reinstated even if the employer must discharge permanent replacement workers.
    C. The employer is under no obligation to reinstate a striker if his/her position has been filled during the strike.
    D. The employer can hire replacement workers only on a temporary basis.

23._
24._
25._

KEY (CORRECT ANSWERS)

1. C		11. B	
2. B		12. C	
3. D		13. B	
4. C		14. C	
5. C		15. D	
6. C		16. B	
7. C		17. D	
8. C		18. B	
9. B		19. C	
10. B		20. C	

21. C
22. A
23. A
24. A
25. C

EXAMINATION SECTION
TEST 1

DIRECTIONS: Each question or incomplete statement is followed by several suggested answers or completions. Select the one that BEST answers the question or completes the statement. *PRINT THE LETTER OF THE CORRECT ANSWER IN THE SPACE AT THE RIGHT.*

1. In Freud's theory, the aspect of personality that operates according to the pleasure principle is called the   1.___
   A. id   B. ego
   C. superego   D. unconditioned stimulus

2. The soundness with which a test measures what it is intended to measure is referred to as its   2.___
   A. validity   B. reliability
   C. positive correlation D. statistical significance

3. When two treatments combine to have an effect that is greater than the sum of the individual treatment effects, we say that there is a _____ effect.   3.___
   A. main   B. synergistic
   C. teratogen   D. developmental systems

4. According to psychologist Kurt Lewin, *There is nothing so practical as a good*   4.___
   A. fact   B. theory
   C. assumption   D. 5-cent cigar

5. A researcher designs a study in which he will give candy to one group of children for breakfast, and eggs and cereal to a second group. He then plans to test the children's physical endurance during gym class at 9:30 in the morning.
   Regarding this study, we can say that the type of food is the   5.___
   A. control variable   B. dependent variable
   C. independent variable D. sample

6. In Pavlov's classic experiments with dogs, the bell was the   6.___
   A. unconditioned stimulus B. conditioned stimulus
   C. unconditioned response D. conditioned response

7. The practice of rooming-in allows the   7.___
   A. father to stay in the hospital room overnight
   B. hospital to double-up on rooms to save costs
   C. mother to stay at home to have the baby
   D. baby to be with the mother whenever the mother wishes

8. Which of the following is a statement fundamental to   8.__
   social learning theory?
   A. Many behaviors are learned gradually through shaping.
   B. Many behaviors are learned quickly through observa-
      tion and imitation (modelling).
   C. The frequency of a desired behavior is affected by
      rewards contingent on the behavior.
   D. Knowledge is constructed as a result of interaction
      between the individual and the environment.

9. The belief that racial mixing results in inferior offspring   9.__
   is contradicted by the idea of
   A. paradigms   B. critical periods
   C. hybrid vigor   D. natural selection

10. Betty Rubin's newborn snuggles near his mom's breast and   10.__
    turns his head several times to find a good nursing posi-
    tion. Just then the phone rings loudly and he startles,
    throws his arms out and loses his comfortable position.
    Which two reflexes are illustrated in order of appearance?
    A. Babinski and Moro   B. Rooting and Moro
    C. Rooting and Babinski   D. Moro and Babinski

11. When looking at theories and applying them, they are NOT   11.__
    A. things that evolve over time
    B. facts
    C. systematic and organized assumptions
    D. affected by the theorist's social context

12. One reason for having a control group in an experimental   12.__
    study is to
    A. keep the children in the experimental group from
       controlling the outcome
    B. check to see if events external to the study made
       the experimental group score high or low
    C. see what happens to children who are initially
       different from the control group
    D. make the experiment a case study

13. A limited time period when rapid development takes place   13.__
    in an organ, a part of the body, or a behavior is referred
    to as a(n)
    A. age of viability   B. developmental pull
    C. critical period   D. pseudodevelopmental phase

14. Mrs. Jann says her new baby wants to learn things just   14.__
    because they are interesting. Who would agree with her?
    A. Freud   B. Skinner   C. Watson   D. Piaget

15. Every gene is a sequence of   15.__
    A. somatic cells   B. trophoblasts
    C. DNA   D. chorionics

16. An individual's tendency to discount information that is   16.___
not consistent with what he or she already believes is an
example of
    A. negation bias   B. confirmatory bias
    C. blind procedure   D. construct validity

17. During the first half of the 20th century, there were a   17.___
number of movements designed to improve humankind by
eliminating, sterilizing, or forbidding marriage to
individuals perceived to be inferior. These are classified as
    A. ego-defense   B. classical conditioning
    C. social interactionist   D. eugenics

18. Reflexes such as rooting, Babinski, Moro, and tonic neck   18.___
    A. develop slowly during the neonatal and infancy periods
    B. replace the voluntary movements made by infants at
       birth
    C. begin to appear after neonates are able to maintain
       a normal body temperature
    D. are typically replaced by voluntary behaviors during
       the first year of life

19. Piaget indicated that babies know about the world through   19.___
their interactions with objects. He called this
    A. object reality
    B. object permanence
    C. sensorimotor intelligence
    D. state interaction

20. Which of the following statements is based on a *behavioral*   20.___
view of child development?
    A. Children seek stimulation.
    B. You may play with your toys after you have cleaned up
       your room.
    C. Children need to work out their emotional conflicts
       through dramatic play.
    D. Leave her alone; she'll grow out of it.

21. Alcohol and cigarette smoke are examples of environmental   21.___
agents that adversely affect prenatal development. They
are called
    A. anoxias   B. perinatals
    C. surrogates   D. teratogens

22. Which of the following is an important focus in the   22.___
development systems approach to child development?
    A. Mutual interaction throughout many levels of organi-
       zation
    B. Neurological maturation
    C. Equilibration
    D. Progression from one stage to the next

23. Which of the following is NOT an example of a social biological effect?
    A
       A. child's exposure to high levels of lead resulting in a lowered IQ
       B. child born with fetal alcohol syndrome
       C. child who develops a fear of dogs after being bitten
       D. man living near Chernobyl whose sperm have chromo-somal damage

23._

24. A child who is learning soccer skills might be guided through the zone of proximal development by
       A. having the child practice with a more skilled peer
       B. receiving a reinforcement for each skill level mastered
       C. exposure to unconditioned stimuli
       D. shaping successive approximations to the target behavior

24._

25. Do infants who sleep separately from their mothers grow up to be more independent than those who sleep with their mothers?
       A. Yes
       B. No
       C. There is no research on this
       D. There is no definitive answer according to research done

25._

KEY (CORRECT ANSWERS)

1. A			11. B	
2. A			12. B	
3. B			13. C	
4. B			14. D	
5. C			15. C	
6. B			16. B	
7. D			17. D	
8. B			18. D	
9. C			19. C	
10. B			20. B	

21. D
22. A
23. C
24. A
25. D

TEST 2

DIRECTIONS: Each question or incomplete statement is followed by several suggested answers or completions. Select the one that BEST answers the question or completes the statement. *PRINT THE LETTER OF THE CORRECT ANSWER IN THE SPACE AT THE RIGHT.*

1. Depth perception is   1.___
   A. formed from concepts   B. learned by habituation
   C. innate   D. modeled from parents

2. Grammatical errors are common in the language of pre-   2.___
   schoolers. Which of the following is appropriate advice
   for how to handle grammatical errors?
   A. Use a direct approach by saying *No*, then telling them
      how they should say the sentence
   B. With each error, ask a question about what the child
      said, using the correct use of the word in the ques-
      tion
   C. Say, *Please try saying that sentence again*
   D. Listen for content and use the correct grammar in
      conversational responses to the child

3. The Chess and Thomas longitudinal study of easy, difficult,   3.___
   and slow-to-warm-up children suggests that the _____ is
   critical for successful child rearing.
   A. goodness-of-fit between child temperament and parental
      interaction styles
   B. genetic temperament of the child matters more than the
      initial parenting style
   C. initial parenting style matters more than the early
      temperament of the child
   D. child's genetics and peer group

4. Preschooler Seth Thomas is counting a dozen blocks on the   4.___
   table. He touches them all, some twice, and ends up with
   a count of 15. What kind of counting error is he making?
   A. Coordination   B. Hierarchical
   C. Partitioning   D. Tagging

5. Which of the following is NOT a good example of functional   5.___
   autonomy?
   A. Brushing your teeth   B. Good manners
   C. Bulimia   D. Breathing

6. Which of the following is most likely to promote locomotor   6.___
   development in 4-month-old infants?
   A. Placing them in a stomach-down prone position on the
      floor
   B. Laying them on their backs and encouraging spontaneous
      leg exercises

C. Providing lots of pillows to permit climbing and more upright positioning

D. Stimulating after 6 months since development isn't facilitated until then

7. The degree to which a 9-month-old exhibits stranger anxiety can be reduced by
   A. the mother being in constant contact with her baby
   B. the child's inability to crawl or walk away
   C. social referencing
   D. social games

8. According to a research study, when mothers brought their babies in for a doctor's examination, it was found that the group of mothers who stood closest to their babies had more early contact with their children. It is difficult to argue that this means that these mothers had bonded better with their children because the outcome measure lacks _____ validity.
   A. predictive
   B. face
   C. external
   D. internal

9. Which of the following are characteristics of infant-directed or child-directed speech (CDS)?
   A. More narrow pitch range
   B. Less contrast between high and low pitches
   C. Longer pauses between words
   D. All of the above

10. According to analysis of Maccoby's study on infants' babbling, does babbling relate to or predict later intelligence?
    A. *Yes*, for boys only
    B. *Yes*, for girls only
    C. *Yes*, for both boys and girls
    D. *No*; when boys and girls are separated, there is no relation

11. Which of the following is the most noticeable change in appearance during the preschool years?
    A. Protruding stomach
    B. Rapid growth of legs and trunk
    C. Fast growth in height
    D. Weight gained faster than during year one

12. During the preschool years, there are many changes in motor development. Which of the following is NOT an accurate statement about motor development changes?
    A. Fine motor development of the fingers allows marked improvement in coloring, cutting, and pasting.
    B. Because their center of gravity moves up, they are more coordinated in climbing and jumping.
    C. Jumping ability improves markedly in part due to thrusting their arms forward rather than *winging* their arms in a jump.
    D. In climbing ladders and jungle gyms, there is a change from marked-time climbing to alternating feet.

13. Which of the following was found to be a productive way
    to overcome attachment difficulties between mothers and
    babies during the first year of life?
    A. Trying to get the baby to imitate the mother's actions
    B. Soliciting the baby's attention when he looked away
    C. Teaching the mother to choose appropriate responses
       to the baby's signals
    D. Teaching the mother to plan a regular schedule of
       activities in order to establish a routine with the
       infant

13.___

14. In number conservation tasks, most preschoolers judge
    which row has more objects by
    A. the length of the row
    B. counting the objects in the display
    C. making another row that is identical to the first and
       counting objects as they make the second row
    D. compensation

14.___

15. By 6 years of age, when most children enter first grade,
    their vocabularies range from about _____ words.
    A. 3,000-6,000   B. 7,000-9,000
    C. 10,000-14,000   D. 15,000-20,000

15.___

16. Baby Shemirah now has the ability to imagine actions in
    her head. Piaget would say that this ability allows a
    strong concept of
    A. object permanence   B. imagination
    C. habituation   D. fixation

16.___

17. A significantly slower than average rate of growth that
    is due to feeding and caregiving problems rather than to
    disease or heredity is termed
    A. encropresis   B. failure-to-thrive
    C. slow-growth syndrome D. maturational lag

17.___

18. Two-month-old baby Watson looks longer at his own mother
    than he does at the occasional sitter, visiting grandma,
    or the bookmobile delivery woman. This recognition is
    based upon his mother's
    A. facial features   B. hairline
    C. eye contact   D. voice cues

18.___

19. At age 11 months, Missy started saying *da-da* rather than
    her usual *dadadada*. According to developmental linguists,
    she is now
    A. overextending   B. babbling
    C. modifying   D. using a protoword

19.___

20. Peter and his younger sister Sally were playing *house*.
    Peter told Sally to set the table while he cooked the
    turkey, showing her how to count the forks and napkins.
    Then he asked her to think of a good desert.

20.___

Peter is _____ his sister's pretend play abilities.
   A. categorizing   B. scaffolding
   C. modeling   D. decentrizing

21. Jill can't take another point of view and tells you what   21.__
    the child sitting on the other side of the mountain can
    see. Piaget would say that she is
       A. hierarchical   B. self-centered
       C. identity-bound   D. egocentric

22. Many 3-year-old children were quite frightened by the   22.__
    dinosaur movie, JURASSIC PARK. The reason is that younger
    children
       A. can't centrate on film
       B. can't distinguish appearance from reality
       C. have highly tuned emotional systems
       D. have too much imagination

23. Which of the following is supported by research on infant   23.__
    and toddler development?
       A. The weight of the brain's cortex is unaffected by
          environmental factors.
       B. It is fairly easy to separate the effects of mal-
          nourishment and stimulation deprivation.
       C. About 10% of the adult's brain weight develops during
          the first two years.
       D. A stimulating environment can produce more growth
          of brain cells.

24. Selma is 3 years old. Her dad has read TEDDY BEAR, TEDDY   24.__
    BEAR to her many times. Now Selma can *read* it aloud with
    inflection, even though she isn't actually reading the
    words. Selma is a(n) _____ reader.
       A. beginning   B. coded
       C. emergent   D. syllabic

25. Which of the following is true concerning hearing problems   25.__
    in infants?
       A. It is difficult for infants to learn sign language.
       B. When deaf children learn sign language, they learn it
          at a slower rate than hearing children learn oral
          language.
       C. If infants make vocal sounds, they must be able to
          hear them.
       D. Infants learning sign language babble in sign just
          as hearing infants babble orally.

KEY (CORRECT ANSWERS)

1. C	6. A	11. B	16. A	21. D
2. D	7. C	12. B	17. B	22. B
3. A	8. B	13. C	18. B	23. D
4. C	9. C	14. A	19. D	24. C
5. D	10. B	15. C	20. B	25. D

TEST 3

DIRECTIONS: Each question or incomplete statement is followed by several suggested answers or completions. Select the one that BEST answers the question or completes the statement. *PRINT THE LETTER OF THE CORRECT ANSWER IN THE SPACE AT THE RIGHT.*

1. Kohlberg called the first level of moral development *preconventional*. At this level, children make moral decisions   1.___
   A. based on what is expected of them by society
   B. based on a simple set of philosophical principles
   C. on the basis of self-interest
   D. on the basis of living up to what close family members expect of them

2. The ability to attend to the form rather than the meaning of language is called   2.___
   A. phonological awareness
   B. metalinguistic awareness
   C. multisyllabic interpretations
   D. word boundary interpretations

3. Emotions can have positive or negative natures. This is called the   3.___
   A. target   B. valence   C. surrogate   D. polarity

4. Which of the following illustrates the secular growth trend?   4.___
   A. April is an Olympic champion in running and hasn't begun her menstrual period, even at age 15.
   B. June is very uncomfortable with her transition to adulthood based mainly on her individual perceptions.
   C. August is beginning her menstrual period at age 11, and her great-grandmother, who didn't begin until 15, is quite concerned.
   D. October is not faring very well in academics or social situations and her doctor wants her checked for secondary characteristics.

5. Carl has not seen the word *unbending* before, but he knows what *bending* means. Since he also understands *un*, he will be able to figure out what *unbending* means by   5.___
   A. understanding the word from its grammatical structure
   B. inferring word meaning from morphological knowledge
   C. learning from the suffix information
   D. getting the meaning from context

6. When Maria finally realizes that she will always be a girl, even if she cuts her hair or changes her clothes, we say she has achieved   6.___
   A. gender identity   B. gender constancy
   C. gender typing   D. sex-role structure

7. Why does Piaget label the thinking of school-age children   7._
as *concrete operational*?
   A. As long as they can see what they are talking about,
      or are familiar with it, they can think logically.
   B. While they cannot think abstractly, they can cement
      abstract ideas together if they make sense.
   C. Since the structure is basic or concrete, the thinking
      process can only be basic.
   D. They can juggle variables and contemplate possibili-
      ties about situations that exist only in their minds.

8. In the 3-kinds-of-memory-store model, which memory is our   8._
working memory?
   A. Sensory   B. Long-term
   C. Short-term   D. Intermediate

9. Carrie, a third grade girl, according to the research on   9._
beliefs and expectations is most likely to
   A. respond to failure by increasing her efforts
   B. believe that when she fails, she can expect more
      reinforcement from her teacher
   C. attribute failure to a lack of ability
   D. attribute her poor performance to nonintellectual
      aspects of her work

10. Race was examined as a risk factor in Sameroff's study   10._
because
   A. research has demonstrated that children from different
      races vary in their risk-taking behavior
   B. race is related to many negative outcomes in our
      society, even if it does not cause them
   C. minority children mature earlier, which puts them
      at risk
   D. experiments have demonstrated a causal relationship
      between race and cognitive performance

11. In regard to socialization and moral development, _____   11._
is the process whereby adult values are adopted as the
child's own, and _____ explains why the child adopts the
characteristics of the same-sex parent.
   A. social responsiveness; proximity seeking
   B. proximity seeking; social responsiveness
   C. identification; internalization
   D. internalization; identification

12. Cleo's dad decided to ignore Cleo's whining about not   12._
wanting to go to bed. Eventually she stopped whining.
One night she smiled as she was putting on her pajamas,
and her dad said, *My, I do like to see those nice bedtime
smiles.* Cleo became happier about bedtime.
Her clever dad first used a(n) _____ procedure, then a(n)
_____ procedure.
   A. social cognition; reinforcement
   B. extinction; reinforcement
   C. extinction; exhortation
   D. social cognition; exhortation

13. Sternberg's triarchic theory of intelligence differenti-   13.___
    ates between which three aspects of mental ability?
    A. Verbal, quantitative, analytical
    B. Analytical, creative, practical
    C. Logical-mathematical, bodily-kinesthetic, inter-
       personal
    D. Memory, convergent, divergent

14. _____ are the primary engines of development.   14.___
    A. Chaos and individualism   B. Continuity and change
    C. Proximal processes   D. Peer groups

15. What is the level of intelligence for most ADHD children?   15.___
    A. Above normal   B. Normal
    C. Below normal   D. No data available

16. Which of the following best describes brain growth during   16.___
    the school-age years?
    A. Brain weight equals adult levels by age 6.
    B. Brain myelination is complete by age 7.
    C. Brain lateralization begins at age 6.
    D. The head grows quickly during the school-age years.

17. Sally is going through tremendous physical changes and   17.___
    is increasing in height and weight very quickly. However,
    she has not yet reached menarche.
    What term do we give to this period of development?
    A. Puberty   B. Juvenescence
    C. Pubescence   D. Presexagesimal

18. Changes that occurred in diary recordings from the late   18.___
    19th century to the early 20th century were from
      I. no explicit sexual content in entries in the 19th
         century to entries discussing heterosexual and homo-
         sexual behaviors in the 20th century
     II. strong family loyalty apparent in entries in the
         19th century to disregard for parents and thoughts
         of running away in the 20th century
    III. entries planning to make alterations in one's charac-
         ter in the 19th century to plans to make alterations
         in one's outer appearances in the 20th century

    The CORRECT answer is:
    A. I *only*   B. II *only*   C. I, III   D. I, II, III

19. Over the course of this century, the ratio of youths to   19.___
    adults has
    A. steadily increased
    B. steadily decreased
    C. both decreased and increased
    D. mirrored the secular growth trend

20. Which of the following is a secondary sex characteristic?   20._
    A. Ovulation   B. Menstruation
    C. Axillary hair   D. Muscle development

21. Some data shows that little girls don't imitate Batman   21._
    and Power Rangers nearly as much as little boys do.
    According to Bandura, this occurs because
        A. girls are innately less aggressive
        B. boys have more imagination
        C. girls don't perceive themselves as similar to the
           models
        D. boys don't want to be perceived as *sissies*

22. Sue's preschool teacher said to her, *You're spending so*   22._
    much time on those drawings and they are so colorful!
    Won't they look nice on the art wall! Sue sees herself
    as an artist, and returns to the painting area every day.
    Her teacher has used
        A. verbal prompting   B. response cost
        C. positive attribution   D. social cognizing

23. Studies of children who have been exposed to violence   23._
    show all but one of the following:
        A. Exposure to violence decreases children's future
           orientation
        B. Real news on television helps children to understand
           that violence is not a major threat
        C. Children's confidence is declining for believing that
           adults can protect them from violence
        D. Children are becoming desensitive to violence

24. What does current research point to as the primary   24._
    problem in dyslexia?
        A. Language processing   B. Vision problems
        C. Visual-motor problems   D. Low intelligence

25. Arnold Sameroff's study of the accumulation of risk   25._
    factors shows that
        A. each accumulation of an additional risk factor in a
           child's environment was related to an equal decrease
           in the child's later IQ
        B. categorical programs are likely to be the most
           successful at dealing with the accumulation of risk
           factors
        C. some risk factors put a child at much greater risk
           for a decreased IQ than others
        D. children with one or two risk factors had only
           slightly lower later IQs than those with no risk
           factors

KEY (CORRECT ANSWERS)

1. C		11. D	
2. B		12. B	
3. B		13. B	
4. C		14. C	
5. B		15. B	
6. B		16. A	
7. A		17. C	
8. C		18. C	
9. C		19. C	
10. B		20. C	

21. C
22. C
23. B
24. A
25. D

EXAMINATION SECTION
TEST 1

DIRECTIONS:
Each question or incomplete statement is followed by several suggested answers or completions. Select the one that *BEST* answers the question or completes the statement. *PRINT THE LETTER OF THE CORRECT ANSWER IN THE SPACE AT THE RIGHT.*

1. When a counselor is planning a future interview with a client, of the following, the *MOST* important consideration is the
    A. recommendations he will make to the client
    B. place where the client will be interviewed
    C. purpose for which the client will be interviewed
    D. personality of the client
    1. ...

2. For a counselor to make a practice of reviewing the client's case record, if available, prior to the interview, is, usually,
    A. *inadvisable,* because knowledge of the client's past record will tend to influence the counselor's judgment
    B. *advisable,* because knowledge of the client's background will help the counselor to identify discrepancies in the client's responses
    C. *inadvisable,* because such review is time-consuming and of questionable value
    D. *advisable,* because knowledge of the client's background will help the counselor to understand the client's situation
    2. ...

3. Assume that a counselor makes a practice of constantly reassuring clients with serious and complex problems by making such statements as: "I'm sure you'll soon be well;" "I know you'll get a job soon;" or "Everything will be all right."
Of the following, the *MOST* likely result of such a practice is to
    A. encourage the client and make him feel that the counselor understands what the client is going through
    B. make the client doubtful about the counselor's understanding of his difficulties and the counselor's ability to help
    C. confuse the client and cause him to hesitate to take any action on his own initiative
    D. help the client to be more realistic about his situation and the probability that it will improve
    3. ...

4. In order to get the maximum amount of information from a client during an interview, of the following, it is *MOST* important for the counselor to communicate to the client the feeling that the counselor is
    A. interested in the client B. a figure of authority
    C. efficient in his work habits
    D. sympathetic to the client's life style
    4. ...

5. Of the following, the counselor who takes extremely detailed notes during an interview with a client is *most likely* to
    A. encourage the client to talk freely
    5. ...

1

    B. distract and antagonize the client
    C. help the client feel at ease
    D. understand the client's feelings

6. As a counselor, you find that many of the clients you   6. ...
interview are verbally abusive and unusually hostile to
you.
Of the following, the *MOST* appropriate action for you to
take *first* is to
    A. review your interviewing techniques and consider
       whether you may be provoking these clients
    B. act in a more authoritative manner when interview-
       ing troublesome clients
    C. tell these clients that you will not process their
       applications unless their troublesome behavior ceases
    D. disregard the clients' troublesome behavior during the
       interview

7. During an interview, you did not completely understand   7. ...
several of your client's responses. In each instance, you
rephrased the client's statement and asked the client if
that was what he meant.
For you to use such a technique during interviews would be
considered
    A. *inappropriate;* you may have distorted the client's
       meaning by rephrasing his statements
    B. *inappropriate;* you should have asked the same question
       until you received a comprehensible response
    C. *appropriate;* the client will have a chance to correct
       you if you have misinterpreted his responses
    D. *appropriate;* a counselor should rephrase clients' re-
       sponses for the records

8. A counselor is interviewing a client who has just had a   8. ...
severe emotional shock because of an assault on her by a
mugger.
Of the following, the approach which would generally be
MOST helpful to the client is for the counselor to
    A. comfort the client and encourage her to talk about
       the assault
    B. sympathize with the client but refuse to discuss
       the assault with her
    C. tell the client to control her emotions and think
       positively about the future
    D. proceed with the interview in an impersonal and un-
       emotional manner

9. A counselor finds that her questions are misinterpreted   9. ...
by many of the clients she interviews.
Of the following, the *MOST* likely reason for this problem
is that the
    A. client is not listening attentively
    B. client wants to avoid the subject being discussed
    C. counselor has failed to express her meaning clearly
    D. counselor has failed to put the client at ease

10. For a counselor to look directly at the client and ob-   10. ...
serve him during the interview is generally
    A. *inadvisable;* this will make the client nervous and
       ·uncomfortable

B. *advisable;* the client will be more likely to refrain
from lying
C. *inadvisable;* the counselor will not be able to take
notes for the case record
D. *advisable;* this will encourage conversation and ac-
celerate the progress of the interview
11. You are interviewing a client who is applying for social   11. ...
services for the first time. In order to encourage this
client to freely give you the information needed for you
to establish his eligibility, of the following, the *BEST*
way to *start* the interview is by
A. asking questions the client can easily answer
B. conveying the impression that his responses to your
questions will be checked
C. asking two or three similar but important questions
D. assuring the client that your sole responsibility is
"getting the facts"
12. Counselors are encouraged to record significant informa-   12. ...
tion obtained from clients and services provided for clients.
Of the following, the *MOST* important reason for this practice
is that these case records will
A. help to reduce the need for regular supervisory con-
ferences
B. indicate to counselors which clients are taking up
the most time
C. provide information which will help the agency to
improve its services to clients
D. make it easier to verify the complaints of clients
13. As a counselor you find that interviews can be completed   13. ...
in a shorter period of time if you ask questions which
limit the client to a certain answer.
For you to use such a technique would be considered
A. *inappropriate,* because this type of question usually
requires advance preparation
B. *inappropriate,* because this type of question may in-
hibit the client from saying what he really means
C. *appropriate,* because you know the areas into which
the questions should be directed
D. *appropriate,* because this type of question usually
helps clients to express themselves clearly
14. Assume that, while you are interviewing an individual   14. ...
to obtain information, the individual pauses in the
middle of an answer.
The *BEST* of the following actions for you to take at
this time is to
A. correct any inaccuracies in what he has said
B. remain silent until he continues
C. explain your position on the matter being discussed
D. explain that time is short and that he must complete
his story quickly
15. You have been assigned to interview the mother of a   15. ...
five-year-old son in her home to get information useful
in locating the child's absent father. During the interview, you notice many serious bruises on the child's arms
and legs, which the mother explains are due to the child's
clumsiness.

3

Of the following, your *BEST* course of action is to
  A. accept the mother's explanation and concentrate on
     getting information which will help you to locate
     the father
  B. advise the mother to have the child examined for a
     medical condition that may be causing his clumsiness
  C. make a surprise visit to the mother later, to see if
     someone is beating the child
  D. complete your interview with the mother and report
     the case to your supervisor for investigation of
     possible child abuse

16. During an interview, the former landlord of an absent   16. ...
    father offers to help you to locate the father if you
    will give the landlord confidential information you have
    on the financial situation of the father.
    Of the following, you should
      A. immediately end the interview with the landlord
      B. urge the landlord to help you but explain that you
         are not permitted to give him confidential information
      C. freely give the landlord the confidential information
         he requests about the father
      D. give the landlord the information only if he promises
         to keep it confidential

17. You feel that your client, a released mental patient, is   17. ...
    not adjusting well to living on his own in an apartment.
    To gather more information, you interview privately his
    next-door neighbor, who claims that the client is creating
    a "disturbance" and speaks of the client in an angry and
    insulting manner.
    Of the following, the *BEST* action for you to take in this
    situation is to
      A. listen patiently to the neighbor to try to get the
         facts about your client's behavior
      B. inform the neighbor that he has no right to speak
         insultingly about a mentally ill person
      C. make an appointment to interview the neighbor some
         other time when he isn't so upset
      D. tell the neighbor that you were not aware of the
         client's behavior and that you will have the client
         moved

18. As a counselor, you are interviewing a client to deter-   18. ...
    mine his eligibility for a work program. Suddenly the
    client begins to shout that he is in no condition to work
    and that you are persecuting him for no reason.
    Of the following, your *BEST* response to this client is to
      A. advise the client to stop shouting or you will call
         for the security guard
      B. wait until the client calms down, then order him to
         come back for another interview
      C. insist that you are not persecuting the client and
         that he must complete the interview
      D. wait until the client calms down, say that you under-
         stand how he feels, and try to continue the interview

4

19. You are interviewing a mother whose 17-year-old son has re-   19. ...
cently been returned home from a mental institution. Although she is willing to care for her son at home, she is
frightened by his strange and sometimes violent behavior
and does not know the best arrangement to make for his
care.
Of the following, your MOST appropriate response to this
mother's problem is to
    A. describe the supportive services and alternatives
       to home care which are available
    B. help her to accept her son's strange and violent be-
       havior
    C. tell her that she will not be permitted to care for
       her son at home if she is frightened by his behavior
    D. convince her that she is not responsible for her son's
       mental condition

20. Assume that you are interviewing an elderly man who comes   20. ...
to the center several times a month to discuss topics with
you which are not related to social services. You realize
that the man is lonely and enjoys these conversations.
Of the following, it would be MOST appropriate to
    A. politely discourage the man from coming in to pass
       the time with you
    B. avoid speaking to this man the next time he comes
       into the center
    C. explore with the client his feelings about joining
       a senior citizens' center
    D. continue to hold these conversations with the man

21. A client you are interviewing tends to ramble on after   21. ...
each response that he gives, so that many clients are
kept waiting.
In this situation, of the following, it would be MOST
advisable to
    A. try to direct the interview, in order to obtain
       the necessary information
    B. reduce the number of questions asked so that you can
       shorten the interview
    C. arrange a second interview for the client so that
       you can give him more time
    D. tell the client that he is wasting everybody's time

22. A non-minority counselor is about to interview a minori-   22. ...
ty client on public assistance for job placement when
the client says: "What does your kind know about my
problems? You've never had to survive out on these
streets."
Of the following, the counselor's MOST appropriate response in this situation is to
    A. postpone the interview until a minority counselor
       is available to interview the client
    B. tell the client that he must cooperate with the
       counselor if he wants to continue receiving public
       assistance
    C. explain to the client the function of the counselor
       in this unit and the services he provides

D. assure the client that you do not have to be a member of a minority group to understand the effects of poverty

23. When you are interviewing someone to obtain information, the BEST of the following reasons for you to repeat certain of his exact words is to
    A. *assure* him that appropriate action will be taken
    B. *encourage* him to elaborate on a point he has made
    C. *assure* him that you agree with his point of view
    D. *encourage* him to switch to another topic of discussion
23. ...

24. You are interviewing a young client who seriously under-estimates the amount of education and training he will require for a certain occupation.
    For you to tell the client that you think he is mistaken would generally be considered
    A. *inadvisable,* because counselors should not express their opinions to clients
    B. *inadvisable,* because clients have the right to self-determination
    C. *advisable,* because clients should generally be alerted to their misconceptions
    D. *advisable,* because counselors should convince clients to adopt a proper life style
24. ...

25. Of the following, the MOST appropriate manner for a counselor to assume during an interview with a patient is
    A. authoritarian   B. paternal
    C. casual   D. businesslike
25. ...

KEY (CORRECT ANSWERS)

1. C	6. A	11. A	16. B	21. A
2. D	7. C	12. C	17. A	22. C
3. B	8. A	13. B	18. D	23. B
4. A	9. C	14. B	19. A	24. C
5. B	10. D	15. D	20. C	25. D

TEST 2

DIRECTIONS:

Each question or incomplete statement is followed by several suggested answers or completions. Select the one that *BEST* answers the question or completes the statement. *PRINT THE LETTER OF THE CORRECT ANSWER IN THE SPACE AT THE RIGHT.*

1. You are interviewing a legally responsible absent father   1. ...
who refuses to make child support payments because he
claims the mother physically abuses the child.
Of the following, the *BEST* way for you to handle this
situation is to tell the father that you
   A. will report his complaint about the mother, but he
      is still responsible for making child support payments
   B. suspect that he is complaining about the mother in
      order to avoid his own responsibility for making child
      support payments
   C. are concerned with his responsibility to make child
      support payments, not with the mother's abuse of the
      child
   D. can not determine his responsibility for making child
      support payments until his complaint about the mother
      is investigated

2. You are interviewing an elderly woman who lives alone   2. ...
to determine her eligibility for homemaker service at
public expense. Though obviously frail and in need of
this service, the woman is not completely cooperative, and
during the interview, is often silent for a considerable
period of time.
Of the following, the *BEST* way for you to deal with these
periods of silence is to
   A. realize that she may be embarrassed to have to apply
      for homemaker service at public expense, and emphasize
      her right to this service
   B. postpone the interview and make an appointment with
      her for a later date, when she may be better able to
      cooperate
   C. explain to the woman that you have many clients to
      interview and need her cooperation to complete the
      interview quickly
   D. recognize that she is probably hiding something and
      begin to ask questions to draw her out

3. During a conference with an adolescent boy at a juvenile   3. ...
detention center, you find out for the first time that he
would prefer to be placed in foster care rather than re-
turn to his natural parents.
To uncover the reasons why the boy dislikes his own home,
of the following, it would be *MOST* advisable for you to
   A. ask the boy a number of short, simple questions about
      his feelings
   B. encourage the boy to talk freely and express his feel-
      ings as best he can
   C. interview the parents and find out why the boy doesn't
      want to live at home
   D. administer a battery of psychological tests in order
      to make an assessment of the boy's problems

7

4. You are interviewing a mother who is applying for Aid to   4. ...
   Families with Dependent Children because the husband has
   deserted the family. The mother becomes annoyed at having
   to answer your questions and tells you to leave her apart-
   ment.
   Which one of the following actions would be *most appropriate*
   to take *FIRST* in this situation?
   A. Return to the office and close the case for lack of
      cooperation
   B. Tell the mother that you will get the information from
      her neighbors if she does not cooperate
   C. Tell the mother that you must stay until you get
      answers to your questions
   D. Explain to the mother the reasons for the interview
      and the consequences of her failure to cooperate

5. A counselor counseling juvenile clients finds that, al-   5. ...
   though he can tolerate most of their behavior, he becomes
   infuriated when they lie to him.
   Of the following, the counselor can *BEST* deal with his
   anger at his clients' lying by
   A. recognizing his feelings of anger and learning to
      control expression of these feelings to his clients
   B. warning his clients that he cannot be responsible
      for his anger when a client lies to him
   C. using will power to suppress his feelings of anger
      when a client lies to him
   D. realizing that lying is a common trait of juveniles
      and not directed against him personally

6. During an interview, one of your clients, a former drug   6. ...
   addict, has expressed an interest in attending a community
   counseling center and resuming his education.
   In this case, the *MOST* appropriate action that you should
   take *FIRST* is to
   A. determine whether this ambition is realistic for a
      former drug addict
   B. send the client's application to a community counsel-
      ing center which provides services to former addicts
   C. ask the client whether he is really motivated or is
      just seeking your approval
   D. encourage and assist the client to take this step,
      since his interest is a positive sign

7. You are interviewing a client who, during previous ap-   7. ...
   pointments, has not responded to your requests for information required to determine his continued eligibility
   for services. On this occasion, the client again offers
   an excuse which you feel is not acceptable.
   For you to advise the client of the probable loss of services because of his lack of cooperation is
   A. *inappropriate,* because the threat to withhold services
      will harm the relationship between counselor and client
   B. *inappropriate,* because counselors should not reveal to
      clients that they do not believe their statements
   C. *appropriate,* because social services are a reward given
      to cooperative clients

   D. *appropriate,* because the counselor should inform
      clients of the consequences of their lack of co-
      operation
8. Assume that you are counselling an adolescent boy in a   8. ...
   juvenile detention center who has been a ringleader in
   smuggling "pot" into the center.
   During your regular interview with this boy, of the follow-
   ing, it would be *advisable* to
   A. tell him you know that he has been involved in smuggling
      pot and that you are trying to understand the reasons
      for his misbehavior
   B. ignore his pot smuggling in order to reassure him that
      you understand and accept him, even though you do not
      agree with his standards of behavior
   C. warn him that you have reported his pot smuggling and
      that he will be punished for his misbehavior
   D. show him that you disapprove of his pot smuggling, but
      assure him that you will not report him for his mis-
      behavior
9. Your unit has received several complaints about a homeless 9. ...
   elderly woman living outdoors in various locations in the
   area. To help determine the need for protective services
   for this woman, you interview several persons in the
   neighborhood who are familiar with her, but all are unco-
   operative or reluctant to give information.
   Of the following, your *BEST* approach to these persons is
   to explain to them that
   A. you will take legal steps against them if they do not
      cooperate with you
   B. their cooperation may enable you to help this home-
      less woman
   C. you need their cooperation to remove this homeless
      woman from their neighborhood
   D. they will be responsible for any harm that comes to
      this homeless woman
10. Assume that you are interviewing a client regarding an   10. ...
    adjustment in budget. The client begins to scream at
    you that she holds you responsible for the decrease in
    her allowance.
    Of the following, *which* is the *BEST* way for you to handle
    this situation?
    A. Attempt to discuss the matter calmly with the client
       and explain her right to a hearing
    B. Urge the client to appeal and assure her of your
       support
    C. Tell the client that her disorderly behavior will be
       held against her
    D. Tell the client that the reduction is "due to red
       tape" and is not your fault
11. As a counselor assigned to a juvenile detention center,   11. ...
    you are having a counselling interview with a recently
    admitted boy who is having serious problems in adjusting
    to confinement in the center. During the interview, the
    boy frequently interrupts to ask you personal questions.

9

Of the following, the *BEST* way for you to deal with these
questions is to
   A. tell him in a friendly way that your job is to dis-
      cuss his problems, not yours
   B. try to understand how the questions relate to the
      boy's own problems and reply with discretion
   C. take no notice of the questions and continue with
      the interview
   D. try to win the boy's confidence by answering his
      questions in detail

12. A counselor is interviewing an elderly woman who hesi-   12. ...
tates to provide necessary information about her finances
to determine whether she is eligible for supplementary
assistance. She fears that this information will be reported to others and that her neighbors will find out that
she is destitute and applying for "welfare."
Of the following, the counselor's *MOST* appropriate response
is to
   A. tell her that, if she hesitates to give this informa-
      tion, the agency will get it from other sources
   B. assure her that this information is kept strictly
      confidential and will not be given to unauthorized
      persons
   C. convince her that her application will be turned down
      unless she provides this information as soon as
      possible
   D. ask for the name and address of her nearest relative
      and obtain the information from that person

13. You are counseling a couple whose children have been   13. ...
placed in a foster home because of the couple's quarreling
and child neglect. When you interview the wife by herself,
she tells you that she knows the husband often "cheats" on
her with other women, but she is too afraid of the husband's
temper to tell him how much this hurts her.
For you to immediately reveal to the husband the wife's
unhappiness concerning his "cheating" is, generally,
   A. *good practice,* because it will help the husband to
      understand why his wife quarrels with him
   B. *poor practice,* because information received from the
      wife should not be given to the husband without her
      permission
   C. *good practice,* because the husband will direct his
      anger at you rather than at his wife
   D. *poor practice,* because the wife may have told you a
      false story about her husband in order to win your
      sympathy

14. A counselor is beginning a job placement interview with   14. ...
a tall, strongly built young man. As the man sits down,
the counselor comments: "I know a big fellow like you
wouldn't be interested in any clerical job."
For the counselor to make such a comment is, generally,
   A. *appropriate,* because it creates an air of familiarity
      which may put the man at ease
   B. *inappropriate,* because the man may be sensitive about
      his physical size

    C. *appropriate,* because the counselor is using his
      judgment to help speed up the interview
    D. *inappropriate,* because the man may feel he is being
      pressured into agreeing with the counselor

15. A counselor in a men's shelter is counseling a middle-   15. ...
    aged client for alcoholism. During counseling, the
    client confesses that, many years ago, he had often en-
    joyed sexually abusing his ten-year-old daughter. The
    counselor tells the client that he personally finds the
    client's behavior "morally disgusting."
    For the counselor to tell the client this is, generally,
    A. *acceptable counseling practice,* because it may encourage
      the client to feel guilty about his behavior
    B. *unacceptable counseling practice,* because the client may
      try to shock the counselor by confessing other similar
      behavior
    C. *acceptable counseling practice,* because "letting off
      steam" in this manner may relieve tension between the
      counselor and the client
    D. *unacceptable counseling practice,* because the client
      may hesitate to discuss his behavior frankly with the
      counselor in the future

16. During an interview, your client, who wants to move to a 16. ...
    larger apartment, asks you to decide on a suitable neighbor-
    hood for her.
    For you to make such a decision for the client would,
    generally, be considered
    A. *appropriate,* because you can save time and expense by
      sharing your knowledge of neighborhoods with the client
    B. *inappropriate,* because counselors should not help
      clients with this type of decision
    C. *appropriate,* because this will help the client to
      develop confidence in her ability to make decisions
    D. *inappropriate,* because the client should be encouraged
      to accept the responsibility of making this decision

17. A client tells you that he is extremely upset by the   17. ...
    treatment that he received from Center personnel at the
    information desk.
    Which of the following is the *BEST* way to handle this
    complaint during the interview?
    A. Explain to the client that he probably misinter-
      preted what occurred at the information desk
    B. Let the client express his feelings and then proceed
      with the interview
    C. Tell the client that you are not concerned with the
      personnel at the information desk
    D. Escort the client to the information desk to find out
      what really happened

18. You are finishing an interview with a client in which   18. ...
    you have explained to her the procedure she must go
    through to apply for income maintenance.
    Of the following, the *BEST* way for you to make sure that
    she has fully understood the procedure is to ask her
    A. whether she feels she has understood your explanation
      of the procedure

B. whether she has any questions to ask you about the procedure

C. to describe the procedure to you in her own words

D. a few questions to test her understanding of the procedure

19. You are interviewing a client in his home as part of your investigation of an anonymous complaint that he has been receiving Medicaid fraudulently. During the interview, the client frequently interrupts your questions to discuss the hardships of his life and the bitterness he feels about his medical condition.
Of the following, the *BEST* way for you to deal with these discussions is to
   A. cut them off abruptly, since the client is probably just trying to avoid answering your questions
   B. listen patiently, since these discussions may be helpful to the client and may give you information for your investigation
   C. remind the client that you are investigating a complaint against him and he must answer directly
   D. seek to gain the client's confidence by discussing any personal or medical problems which you yourself may have

19. ...

20. While interviewing an absent father to determine his ability to pay child supprt, you realize that his answers to some of your questions contradict his answers to other questions.
Of the following, the *BEST* way for you to try to get accurate information from the father is to
   A. confront him with his contradictory answers and demand an explanation from him
   B. use your best judgment as to which of his answers are accurate and question him accordingly
   C. tell him that he has misunderstood your questions and that he must clarify his answers
   D. ask him the same questions in different words and follow up his answers with related questions

20. ...

21. The one of the following types of interviewees who presents the *LEAST* difficult problem to handle is the person who
   A. answers with a great many qualifications
   B. talks at length about unrelated subjects so that the counselor cannot ask questions
   C. has difficulty understanding the counselor's vocabulary
   D. breaks into the middle of sentences and completes them with a meaning of his own

21. ...

22. A man being interviewed is entitled to Medicaid, but he refuses to sign up for it because he says he cannot accept any form of welfare.
Of the following, the *BEST* course of action to take *FIRST* is to
   A. try to discover the reason for his feeling this way
   B. tell him that he should be glad financial help is available

22. ...

12

C. explain that others cannot help him if he will not
   help himself
D. suggest that he speak to someone who is already on
   Medicaid

23. Of the following, the outcome of an interview by a   23. ...
    counselor depends *MOST* heavily on the
    A. personality of the interviewee
    B. personality of the counselor
    C. subject matter of the questions asked
    D. interaction between counselor and interviewee

24. Some clients being interviewed are primarily interested   24. ...
    in making a favorable impression. The counselor should
    be aware of the fact that such clients are *more likely*
    than other clients to
    A. try to anticipate the answers the interviewer is
       looking for
    B. answer all questions openly and frankly
    C. try to assume the role of interviewer
    D. be anxious to get the interview over as quickly as
       possible

25. The type of interview which a counselor usually con-   25. ...
    ducts is substantially different from most interviewing
    situations in all of the following aspects *EXCEPT* the
    A. setting   B. kinds of clients
    C. techniques employed   D. kinds of problems

KEY (CORRECT ANSWERS)

1. A		11. B	
2. A		12. B	
3. B		13. B	
4. D		14. D	
5. A		15. D	
6. D		16. D	
7. D		17. B	
8. A		18. C	
9. B		19. B	
10. A		20. D	

21. C
22. A
23. D
24. A
25. C

ANSWER SHEET

ST NO. _____ PART _____ TITLE OF POSITION _____

(AS GIVEN IN EXAMINATION ANNOUNCEMENT - INCLUDE OPTION, IF ANY)

ACE OF EXAMINATION _____ DATE _____

(CITY OR TOWN)   (STATE)

RATING

USE THE SPECIAL PENCIL. MAKE GLOSSY BLACK MARKS.

#	A B C D E	#	A B C D E	#	A B C D E	#	A B C D E	#	A B C D E
1	:: :: :: :: ::	26	:: :: :: :: ::	51	:: :: :: :: ::	76	:: :: :: :: ::	101	:: :: :: :: ::
2	:: :: :: :: ::	27	:: :: :: :: ::	52	:: :: :: :: ::	77	:: :: :: :: ::	102	:: :: :: :: ::
3	:: :: :: :: ::	28	:: :: :: :: ::	53	:: :: :: :: ::	78	:: :: :: :: ::	103	:: :: :: :: ::
4	:: :: :: :: ::	29	:: :: :: :: ::	54	:: :: :: :: ::	79	:: :: :: :: ::	104	:: :: :: :: ::
5	:: :: :: :: ::	30	:: :: :: :: ::	55	:: :: :: :: ::	80	:: :: :: :: ::	105	:: :: :: :: ::
6	:: :: :: :: ::	31	:: :: :: :: ::	56	:: :: :: :: ::	81	:: :: :: :: ::	106	:: :: :: :: ::
7	:: :: :: :: ::	32	:: :: :: :: ::	57	:: :: :: :: ::	82	:: :: :: :: ::	107	:: :: :: :: ::
8	:: :: :: :: ::	33	:: :: :: :: ::	58	:: :: :: :: ::	83	:: :: :: :: ::	108	:: :: :: :: ::
9	:: :: :: :: ::	34	:: :: :: :: ::	59	:: :: :: :: ::	84	:: :: :: :: ::	109	:: :: :: :: ::
10	:: :: :: :: ::	35	:: :: :: :: ::	60	:: :: :: :: ::	85	:: :: :: :: ::	110	:: :: :: :: ::

Make only ONE mark for each answer.   Additional and stray marks may be
counted as mistakes.   In making corrections, erase errors COMPLETELY.

#	A B C D E	#	A B C D E	#	A B C D E	#	A B C D E	#	A B C D E
11	:: :: :: :: ::	36	:: :: :: :: ::	61	:: :: :: :: ::	86	:: :: :: :: ::	111	:: :: :: :: ::
12	:: :: :: :: ::	37	:: :: :: :: ::	62	:: :: :: :: ::	87	:: :: :: :: ::	112	:: :: :: :: ::
13	:: :: :: :: ::	38	:: :: :: :: ::	63	:: :: :: :: ::	88	:: :: :: :: ::	113	:: :: :: :: ::
14	:: :: :: :: ::	39	:: :: :: :: ::	64	:: :: :: :: ::	89	:: :: :: :: ::	114	:: :: :: :: ::
15	:: :: :: :: ::	40	:: :: :: :: ::	65	:: :: :: :: ::	90	:: :: :: :: ::	115	:: :: :: :: ::
16	:: :: :: :: ::	41	:: :: :: :: ::	66	:: :: :: :: ::	91	:: :: :: :: ::	116	:: :: :: :: ::
17	:: :: :: :: ::	42	:: :: :: :: ::	67	:: :: :: :: ::	92	:: :: :: :: ::	117	:: :: :: :: ::
18	:: :: :: :: ::	43	:: :: :: :: ::	68	:: :: :: :: ::	93	:: :: :: :: ::	118	:: :: :: :: ::
19	:: :: :: :: ::	44	:: :: :: :: ::	69	:: :: :: :: ::	94	:: :: :: :: ::	119	:: :: :: :: ::
20	:: :: :: :: ::	45	:: :: :: :: ::	70	:: :: :: :: ::	95	:: :: :: :: ::	120	:: :: :: :: ::
21	:: :: :: :: ::	46	:: :: :: :: ::	71	:: :: :: :: ::	96	:: :: :: :: ::	121	:: :: :: :: ::
22	:: :: :: :: ::	47	:: :: :: :: ::	72	:: :: :: :: ::	97	:: :: :: :: ::	122	:: :: :: :: ::
23	:: :: :: :: ::	48	:: :: :: :: ::	73	:: :: :: :: ::	98	:: :: :: :: ::	123	:: :: :: :: ::
24	:: :: :: :: ::	49	:: :: :: :: ::	74	:: :: :: :: ::	99	:: :: :: :: ::	124	:: :: :: :: ::
25	:: :: :: :: ::	50	:: :: :: :: ::	75	:: :: :: :: ::	100	:: :: :: :: ::	125	:: :: :: :: ::

ANSWER SHEET

TEST NO. _____ PART _____ TITLE OF POSITION _____

PLACE OF EXAMINATION _____ DATE _____

(CITY OR TOWN)   (STATE)

RATING

USE THE SPECIAL PENCIL.   MAKE GLOSSY BLACK MARKS.

	A B C D E		A B C D E		A B C D E		A B C D E		A B C D E
1	:: :: :: :: ::	26	:: :: :: :: ::	51	:: :: :: :: ::	76	:: :: :: :: ::	101	:: :: :: :: ::
2	:: :: :: :: ::	27	:: :: :: :: ::	52	:: :: :: :: ::	77	:: :: :: :: ::	102	:: :: :: :: ::
3	:: :: :: :: ::	28	:: :: :: :: ::	53	:: :: :: :: ::	78	:: :: :: :: ::	103	:: :: :: :: ::
4	:: :: :: :: ::	29	:: :: :: :: ::	54	:: :: :: :: ::	79	:: :: :: :: ::	104	:: :: :: :: ::
5	:: :: :: :: ::	30	:: :: :: :: ::	55	:: :: :: :: ::	80	:: :: :: :: ::	105	:: :: :: :: ::
6	:: :: :: :: ::	31	:: :: :: :: ::	56	:: :: :: :: ::	81	:: :: :: :: ::	106	:: :: :: :: ::
7	:: :: :: :: ::	32	:: :: :: :: ::	57	:: :: :: :: ::	82	:: :: :: :: ::	107	:: :: :: :: ::
8	:: :: :: :: ::	33	:: :: :: :: ::	58	:: :: :: :: ::	83	:: :: :: :: ::	108	:: :: :: :: ::
9	:: :: :: :: ::	34	:: :: :: :: ::	59	:: :: :: :: ::	84	:: :: :: :: ::	109	:: :: :: :: ::
10	:: :: :: :: ::	35	:: :: :: :: ::	60	:: :: :: :: ::	85	:: :: :: :: ::	110	:: :: :: :: ::

Make only ONE mark for each answer.   Additional and stray marks may be counted as mistakes.   In making corrections, erase errors COMPLETELY.

	A B C D E		A B C D E		A B C D E		A B C D E		A B C D E
11	:: :: :: :: ::	36	:: :: :: :: ::	61	:: :: :: :: ::	86	:: :: :: :: ::	111	:: :: :: :: ::
12	:: :: :: :: ::	37	:: :: :: :: ::	62	:: :: :: :: ::	87	:: :: :: :: ::	112	:: :: :: :: ::
13	:: :: :: :: ::	38	:: :: :: :: ::	63	:: :: :: :: ::	88	:: :: :: :: ::	113	:: :: :: :: ::
14	:: :: :: :: ::	39	:: :: :: :: ::	64	:: :: :: :: ::	89	:: :: :: :: ::	114	:: :: :: :: ::
15	:: :: :: :: ::	40	:: :: :: :: ::	65	:: :: :: :: ::	90	:: :: :: :: ::	115	:: :: :: :: ::
16	:: :: :: :: ::	41	:: :: :: :: ::	66	:: :: :: :: ::	91	:: :: :: :: ::	116	:: :: :: :: ::
17	:: :: :: :: ::	42	:: :: :: :: ::	67	:: :: :: :: ::	92	:: :: :: :: ::	117	:: :: :: :: ::
18	:: :: :: :: ::	43	:: :: :: :: ::	68	:: :: :: :: ::	93	:: :: :: :: ::	118	:: :: :: :: ::
19	:: :: :: :: ::	44	:: :: :: :: ::	69	:: :: :: :: ::	94	:: :: :: :: ::	119	:: :: :: :: ::
20	:: :: :: :: ::	45	:: :: :: :: ::	70	:: :: :: :: ::	95	:: :: :: :: ::	120	:: :: :: :: ::
21	:: :: :: :: ::	46	:: :: :: :: ::	71	:: :: :: :: ::	96	:: :: :: :: ::	121	:: :: :: :: ::
22	:: :: :: :: ::	47	:: :: :: :: ::	72	:: :: :: :: ::	97	:: :: :: :: ::	122	:: :: :: :: ::
23	:: :: :: :: ::	48	:: :: :: :: ::	73	:: :: :: :: ::	98	:: :: :: :: ::	123	:: :: :: :: ::
24	:: :: :: :: ::	49	:: :: :: :: ::	74	:: :: :: :: ::	99	:: :: :: :: ::	124	:: :: :: :: ::
25	:: :: :: :: ::	50	:: :: :: :: ::	75	:: :: :: :: ::	100	:: :: :: :: ::	125	:: :: :: :: ::